Famous Letters

Famous Letters

MESSAGES & THOUGHTS
THAT SHAPED OUR WORLD

Edited by Frank McLynn

Reader's Digest

THE READER'S DIGEST ASSOCIATION, INC.
Pleasantville, New York/Montreal

CONTENTS

Saint Jerome, biblical scholar, who describes with horror the sack of Rome, when the "bright light of all the world" was put out.

Virginia Woolf, beautiful and talented author, who writes to her future husband revealing her feelings of despair and doubts about the marriage.

Editors Candida Hunt
  Stuart McCready
  Elizabeth Toppin
Art editor Steve McCurdy
Designers Martin Anderson
  Jerry Goldie
  Ayala Kingsley
  Frankie Wood
Picture research management
  Joanne Rapley
Picture researchers Susan Trangmar
  Suzanne Williams
Researchers Lauren Bourque
  Ann Furtado
  Helen McCurdy
Proofreader Lin Thomas
Project editor Peter Furtado
Project management Graham Bateman
Production Stephen Elliott

A READER'S DIGEST BOOK

Produced and prepared by
Andromeda Oxford Ltd.

The acknowledgments that appear
on pp. 156–58 are hereby made a
part of the copyright page.

Copyright © 1993 Andromeda
Oxford Ltd.

Library of Congress Cataloging in Publication Data

Famous letters : messages & thoughts that shaped our world / edited by
  Frank McLynn.
    p.   cm.
  Includes index.
  ISBN 0-89577-521-2
    1. Letters.   I. McLynn, F. J.
  PN6131.F32 1993
808.86—dc20
                                                              93-5848

Reader's Digest and the Pegasus logo
are registered trademarks of The
Reader's Digest Association, Inc.

Printed in Spain by Fournier A. Graficas S. A.

Louis XIV, unforgiving king of France, who wrote to his chief minister warning him not to question the judgment of the monarch.

Death of N Battle of Traf

Nelson's life saved by his Coxswain.

Blockade of Cadiz.

Nelson receiving the Spanish Officers Swords, on board the San Josef.

"Westminster Abbey or Victory" Battle of Cape St Vincent.

the Bear.

This cartoon depicts the life of Nelson, whose last written words were to the woman he loved.

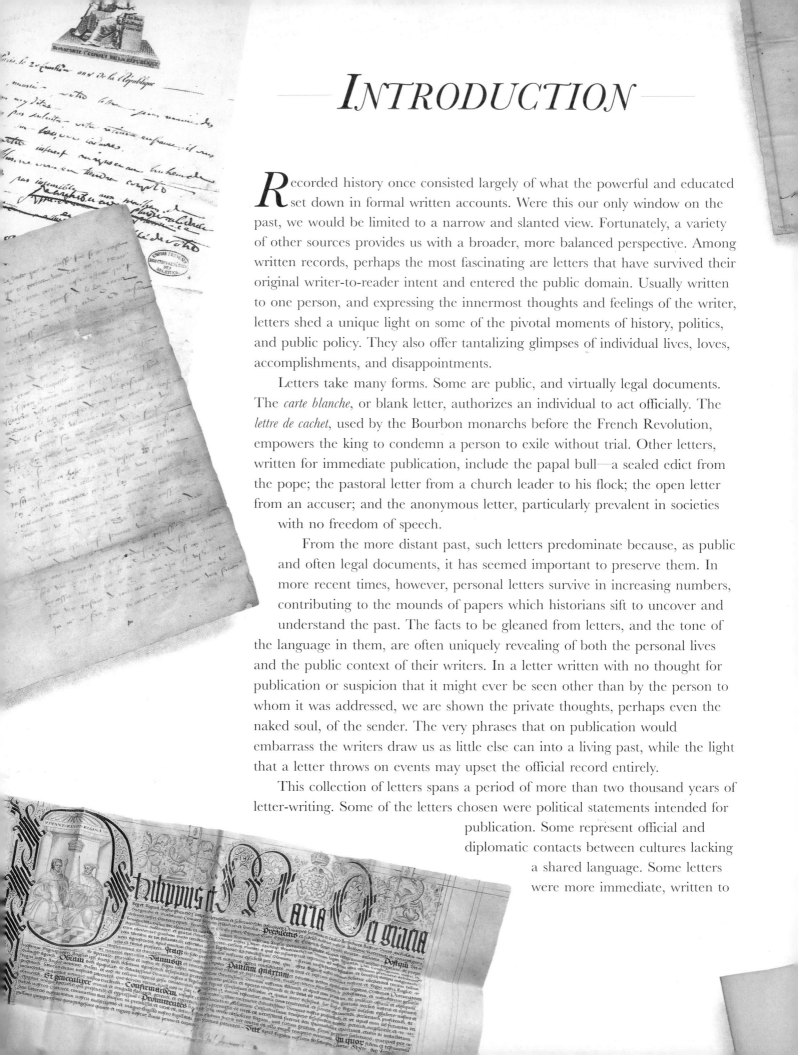

INTRODUCTION

Recorded history once consisted largely of what the powerful and educated set down in formal written accounts. Were this our only window on the past, we would be limited to a narrow and slanted view. Fortunately, a variety of other sources provides us with a broader, more balanced perspective. Among written records, perhaps the most fascinating are letters that have survived their original writer-to-reader intent and entered the public domain. Usually written to one person, and expressing the innermost thoughts and feelings of the writer, letters shed a unique light on some of the pivotal moments of history, politics, and public policy. They also offer tantalizing glimpses of individual lives, loves, accomplishments, and disappointments.

Letters take many forms. Some are public, and virtually legal documents. The *carte blanche*, or blank letter, authorizes an individual to act officially. The *lettre de cachet*, used by the Bourbon monarchs before the French Revolution, empowers the king to condemn a person to exile without trial. Other letters, written for immediate publication, include the papal bull—a sealed edict from the pope; the pastoral letter from a church leader to his flock; the open letter from an accuser; and the anonymous letter, particularly prevalent in societies with no freedom of speech.

From the more distant past, such letters predominate because, as public and often legal documents, it has seemed important to preserve them. In more recent times, however, personal letters survive in increasing numbers, contributing to the mounds of papers which historians sift to uncover and understand the past. The facts to be gleaned from letters, and the tone of the language in them, are often uniquely revealing of both the personal lives and the public context of their writers. In a letter written with no thought for publication or suspicion that it might ever be seen other than by the person to whom it was addressed, we are shown the private thoughts, perhaps even the naked soul, of the sender. The very phrases that on publication would embarrass the writers draw us as little else can into a living past, while the light that a letter throws on events may upset the official record entirely.

This collection of letters spans a period of more than two thousand years of letter-writing. Some of the letters chosen were political statements intended for publication. Some represent official and diplomatic contacts between cultures lacking a shared language. Some letters were more immediate, written to report a discovery, to stir men to action, to right a wrong, or to resist a foe. Others were intimate communications between friends or enemies. Still others were attempts by men and women in trouble to justify themselves to their friends, or to posterity.

The fact that letters have the power to justify behavior and to expose motives gives them the power to influence events and even to change history. Dramatists and novelists often exploit this and make a letter the turning point in a plot. The historian Tacitus described an instance from imperial Rome of a letter from the emperor Tiberius that arrived at the Roman Senate. It was read to the assembled senators, first praising the emperor's favorite Sejanus, then turning into an impassioned denunciation of him, and ending with his death sentence. The dramatic power of the letter has given rise to the fabrication, or falsification, of the form: some ancient historians spiced their narratives with fictional letters to sway the reader's view. Just as those close to a well-known figure may suppress any letters that present their hero in a dubious light, so a person's enemies can spread a spurious picture by circulating false letters. To put something in writing has long been recognized as a sign of personal commitment, and the signature at the end of a letter establishes responsibility for its content. Some of the most poignant letters in this collection, such as that written by the French queen Marie Antoinette to her sister-in-law hours before the queen's execution, were attacked as forgeries by enemies of the writer.

This collection has been made with an eye both to informing and entertaining the reader, and to demonstrating the range of letter writing, in period, geography, and intent. The letters themselves are presented, often in shortened form and rendered into modern English with modern punctuation, to make the message as accessible to the modern reader as it was to the writer's contemporaries.

Raymond Chandler once said: "By nature, a letter is a hybrid (part autobiography, part confessional, part report, part journal, part conversation), and a good letter tames the hybrid, even turning it into art. A good letter is an act of generosity: it uses the voice its writer thinks with, the voice he talks aloud to himself with." This carefully chosen assortment of letters seeks to take the reader right to the moment of writing, and to allow those voices from the past to speak again.

ENCOUNTERS
&
DISCOVERIES

When Neil Armstrong set foot on the Moon in July 1969, his message to the world, "that's one small step for a man, one giant leap for mankind," was instantly relayed back to Earth and broadcast simultaneously all around the globe. Earlier explorers did not enjoy such immediacy or ease of communication with their own bases; before the invention of the radio, contact with pioneers journeying into the unknown depended almost exclusively on the highly unreliable and slow medium of the letter.

On his return journey from his first voyage to what he thought was the fabled land of Cipangu in February 1493, Christopher Columbus feared that his ship would be sunk in a storm. He wrote a letter, wrapped it in oilskin, placed it in a coconut shell and threw it into the sea, in the forlorn hope that it might one day be found and read. Columbus did return to Spain safely, and his final signed account of his achievements was more in the mold of the scientist's report of the new worlds of knowledge to be opened up; it was officially copied by the king and queen of Spain and circulated among interested people.

In the years before the advent of the scientific journal, scientists often reported their inventions and discoveries in personal letters to others working in their field who, they knew, could validate and support the discovery. Thus, long before he formally published his findings, Galileo announced in letters to associates his discovery of planetary secrets by use of his telescope. Likewise Benjamin Franklin, one of the greatest scientists of the 18th century, wrote to Sir Joseph Banks, the equally great botanist and head of the British Royal Society, to report on the far-reaching implications of the new technology of hot-air ballooning developed in Paris in the 1780's.

Albert Einstein, too, used the formula of the signed letter, this time to the president of the United States, to draw attention to the political implications of the atomic knowledge that was burgeoning within the nuclear physicist community in the 1930's. Interestingly, Einstein himself had not written the letter, but his world-famous signature on it gave unique credence and urgency to the message of concern about the future of the world.

Explorers and scientists could report in letters, more or less objectively, on their findings. Some private letters provide the other side of the coin: the fascinating perspective of an individual's personal view on some momentous event in history. Thus we learn, through Pasteur's letter to his children, about the newly discovered medical marvel of inoculation. We can also look through the eyes of Pepys at 17th-century London smitten by the deadly plague, or hear Saint Jerome tell a friend of the horrible sacking of Rome.

Far more difficult than the simple writing of a letter to a friend or loved one was the exchange of letters in diplomatic encounters, taking place in dangerous circumstances and with the parties facing the additional burdens of interpreting the strange language and cultural meanings of their inter-locutors. Exchanges between Qianlong and King George of England, or between the Mongol emperor Kuyuk and the pope, relied on brave (or fool-hardy) ambassadors traveling to the heart of the enemy country. Other ambassadors, such as Commodore Perry, carrying a message from the president of the United States to the Japanese emperor, traveled more secure ground, backed up by superior military might. In every case, the letter form added weight and authority to these communications, destined to direct the flow of human events.

SAINT JEROME
— TO —
EUSTOCHIUM

A.D. 412

*The great Roman scholar and teacher
tells of his shock at the news of the sack
of Rome by barbarians.*

*Saint Jerome. A 17th-century
impression by the French
painter, Georges de la Tour.*

*Top: 5th-
century
Germanic iron
spearheads.*

The fall of Rome, the Eternal City, undefeated by any foreign foe for nearly 800 years, sent shock waves around the Roman world. The news reached Palestine, where the great biblical scholar Saint Jerome was head of a monastery in Bethlehem and at that time engaged in preparing commentaries on Old Testament books. He wrote a prologue to some commentaries in the form of a letter to an old student or friend, and often expressed urgent fears about his life and times.

Saint Jerome was, in 410, famous as a role model for the monastic life. Born in Dalmatia, the coastal area of present-day Croatia, he had been highly educated in rhetoric and the classics at Rome. After experiencing a vision he spent three years as a hermit in the Syrian desert. His achievements as a scholar and translator were prodigious: in addition to his Old Testament commentaries, he produced the first standard Latin text of the Bible. Though he was an austere, iras-

*Left: The Aurelian wall, more
than 12 miles long, was built
around Rome to keep out the
barbarians.*

cible man and contemptuous of those who disagreed with him, he enjoyed a remarkable popularity with women. When he left Rome in 385 after three years as the head of a theological "school" frequented by a group of dedicated Christian women, the wealthy widow Paula accompanied him to Palestine. In Bethlehem she established a monastery for Saint Jerome, under his direction, and a convent, which she headed herself.

Ten years after Jerome left Rome the emperor Theodosius died and the empire was divided between his sons. Arcadius ruled in the east and Honorius in the west. The effective ruler in Italy was Honorius' general Stilicho, who failed to deal

---

Biography

Saint Jerome (about 341–420), properly Eusebius Hieronymus, was born at Strido, Dalmatia, studied at Rome (where he was baptized), then traveled in the East. After a dangerous illness in Antioch, he retired in 374–78 to the desert of Chalcis and then, in 379, was ordained priest. In 382 he went to Rome on a mission, and stayed on for four years as secretary to Pope Damasus. He settled down permanently in 386 at Bethlehem, where he headed a monastery. He translated the Old Testament from Hebrew into Latin, and revised the Latin translation of the New Testament. Jerome was the most learned and eloquent of all the early Church fathers.

Having completed the eighteen books of the exposition of Isaiah, I was very desirous, Eustochium, Christ's virgin, to go on to Ezekiel, in accordance with my frequent promises to you and your mother Paula, of saintly memory, and thus, as the saying is, put the finishing touches to the work on the prophets. But alas! I was suddenly told of the death of Pammachius and Marcella, the siege of Rome, and the falling asleep of many of my brethren and sisters. I was so stupefied and dismayed that day and night I could think of nothing but the welfare of the community; it seemed as though I was sharing the captivity of the saints, and I could not open my lips until I knew something more definite. All the while, full of anxiety, I was wavering between hope and despair, and was torturing myself with the misfortunes of other people. But when the bright light of all the world was put out, or, rather, when the Roman Empire was decapitated, and, to speak more correctly, the whole world perished in one city, I became dumb and humbled myself, and kept silence from good words, but my grief broke out afresh, my heart glowed within me, and while I meditated the fire was kindled.

Who would believe that Rome, built up by the conquest of the whole world, had collapsed, that the mother of nations had become also their tomb; that the shores of the whole East, of Egypt, of Africa, which once belonged to the imperial city, were filled with the hosts of her men-servants and maid-servants, that we should every day be receiving in this holy Bethlehem men and women who once were noble and abounding in every kind of wealth, but are now reduced to poverty? We cannot relieve these sufferers: all we can do is to sympathize with them, and unite our tears with theirs. The burden of this holy work was as much as we could carry; the sight of the wanderers, coming in crowds, caused us deep pain; and we therefore abandoned the exposition of Ezekiel, and almost all study, and were filled with a longing to turn the words of Scripture into action, and not to say holy things but to do them. Now, however, in response to your admonition, Eustochium, Christ's virgin, we resume the interrupted labor, and approach our third Book.

JEROME

with the growing power of the Visigoths. Before his death, Theodosius had permitted the Visigoths (Germanic peoples) under their king, Alaric, to settle within Roman borders.

The German invasion of Gaul (France) in 406 lost Rome that province, and Alaric used the opportunity to demand money and land from Rome. He was rejected, but marched his army to Rome's gates three years in succession. The gates were opened in treachery to admit him (410), but little destruction occurred, for Alaric was a Christian who forbade the looting of religious buildings.

Above: Stilicho, the defending general.

Left: A Germanic warrior on horseback, from a 7th-century Saxon gravestone.

KUYUK, MONGOL KHAN
TO
POPE INNOCENT IV

1246

*The supreme Mongol ruler, confident
of his might, gives a resounding answer to a
letter from the pope.*

*Kuyuk, khan of
all the khans,
who instructed
Innocent to
"come tender us
service and pay
us homage."*

*Innocent IV,
who claimed
sovereignty over
all earthly
kings, including
"the king of the
Tartars."*

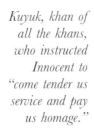he rise of the Mongol empire is one of the most sensational phenomena in world history. Temujin, better known as Genghis Khan, chief of an obscure clan of Asiatic nomads, within a single lifetime (about 1162–1227) and by virtue of military genius alone, became ruler of an empire that stretched from the Black Sea to the Pacific. His son and successor Ogodei (1185–1241) carried on his work of conquest. After sweeping through Russia, the great Mongol generals Batu and Subedei planned the invasion of Europe, launching their armies in a two-pronged attack in 1240.

This advance came to an abrupt halt when Ogodei suddenly died. Batu and Subedei were summoned back to Karakorum in Mongolia for a *kuriltai*, "great council," to elect a successor. Dynastic disputes led to delays, and it was not until 1246 that Kuyuk, eldest son of Ogodei, was chosen as the third khakhan (khan of all the khans), the supreme Mongol ruler.

In the meantime, Pope Innocent IV sent a letter to "the king of the Tartars," exhorting him to abstain from attacking Christians, and threatening him otherwise with the wrath of God in this life and damnation in the next.

Biography

Kuyuk, also spelled Guyuk, (1206–1248), grandson of Genghis Khan, assumed supreme power of the Mongol empire in 1246. Kuyuk's reign lasted less than two years. Strict, arrogant, and unsmiling, he was a harsh and unapproachable ruler, who personally supervised everything, never forgave a wrong, was severe toward corruption and incompetence, and never addressed anyone directly. He died, probably of cirrhosis, while on his way west to wage a war against Batu, who had set himself up as the first khan of the Golden Horde. This breakaway khanate proved to be the longest lived of the divided Mongol empires, and left a permanent imprint on the history of Russia.

*The Mongol
horseman—his
cavalry skills gave
the khan all the
lands "from
sunrise to
sunset."*

By the power of the Eternal Heaven, we are the all-embracing Khan of all the great nations. It is our command: This is a decree, sent to the great Pope that he may know and pay heed.

After holding counsel with the monarchs under your suzerainty, you have sent us an offer of subordination, which we have accepted from the hands of your envoy. You have said it would be well for us to become Christians. You write to me in person about this matter, and have addressed a request to me. This we cannot understand. When you say: "I am a Christian. I pray to God . . ." how do you know who is pleasing to God and to whom he allots his grace? How can you know it, that you speak such words? Thanks to the power of the Eternal Heaven, all lands have been given to us from sunrise to sunset. How could anyone act other than in accordance with the commands of Heaven? Now your own upright heart must tell you: "We will become subject to you, and will place our powers at your disposal." You in person, at the head of the monarchs, all of you, without exception, must come to tender us service and pay us homage, then only will we recognize your submission. But if you do not obey the commands of Heaven, and run counter to our orders, we shall know that you are our foe.

That is what we have to tell you. If you fail to act in accordance with this, how can we foresee what will happen to you? Heaven alone knows.

KUYUK

Left: Letters from the khan bore his seal, stamped in red.

Right: Mongol stirrups, highly effective, were mere loops of leather.

The envoys of the pope, a delegation of Franciscan friars under Giovanni Piano Carpini, later archbishop of Antivari, spent two years (1245–47) on their mission. Carpini was handed on from one local ruler to another until he came to Kiev. He and his companions pressed on by sledge through the Russian winter to Batu's camp beside the river Volga. Batu, locked in a struggle for the succession with Kuyuk, read the letter but would not take responsibility for answering it. He sent Carpini on with just one Franciscan friar to the kuriltai at Karakorum. They arrived 17 months and 3,000 miles after leaving Rome, and were kept waiting until winter, when Kuyuk was confirmed as the new khakhan. He then swiftly gave the answer excerpted above. Its meaning was clear, especially with the warning: "How can we foresee what will happen to you? Heaven alone knows."

Indeed, Heaven alone knew. The dreaded Mongol empire was weakened by civil war and dynastic struggles, saving Europe from further visitations.

CHRISTOPHER COLUMBUS
TO
LUIS DE SANTANGEL

February 15, 1493

*The first European to report
from the Caribbean tells of
the wealth and pleasures of the islands.*

*Christopher Columbus, who
died still believing he had
sailed to India.*

On Friday August 3, 1492, Christopher Columbus set sail from the bar of Saltes, an island near Palos, Spain. He commanded three ships: the *Santa María*, crewed by 50 men, and two smaller caravels, the *Niña* and the *Pinta*. The whole squadron comprised just 120 men. The voyage was the culmination of seven years' negotiations with the king and queen of Spain, Ferdinand and Isabella, and of Columbus's 18-year-old dream that he could sail west across the Atlantic Ocean and so come to the island of Cipangu (Japan) of which Marco Polo had spoken; Polo claimed Japan was 1,500 miles east of Cathay (China).

After calling in at the Canary Islands, Columbus sailed west into the unknown. By October 10, he and his men had doubled all records for ocean sailing and were long past the point where Columbus had said land would be found. Fear pushed his men close to mutiny. The course of history might well have been different had they not caught sight of flocks of petrels flying overhead in a southwesterly direction. With courage renewed and the trade winds bearing them at speed westward, Columbus and his sailors continued until, on October 11, they saw drifting branches and canes. Land itself was sighted on October 12, and landfall made later that day on an island which the native inhabitants called Guanhani. Thinking he had reached India, Columbus called the indigenous people "Indians." Columbus sailed

Biography

Christopher Columbus (1451–1506), whose coat of arms appears right, was born in Genoa, Italy. When he was 14 years old he went to sea; later he conceived an ambition to reach India by sailing westward. He made voyages to Sierra Leone and Cape Verde to turn himself into a master mariner. Not until 1492 did he make his triumphant discovery of the Caribbean. He made voyages in 1493–96, 1498, and, when he sailed to the coast of South America, in 1502–04. Convinced that he had found not a new continent but a new way to India, he died at Valladolid, in Spain.

Above: 14th-century woodcut of a caravel like the Niña and Pinta.

Far right: A globe of the early 1490's by the Dutch cartographer Martin Behaim.

As I know that you will have pleasure of the great victory which our Lord hath given me in my voyage, I write you this, by which you shall know that, in twenty days I passed over to the Indies, where I found very many islands peopled with inhabitants beyond number. There could be no believing, without seeing, such harbors as are here, as well as the many and great rivers, and excellent waters, most of which contain gold. In the trees and fruits and plants, there are great differences from those of Juana. In this, there are many spiceries, and great mines of gold and other metals. The people of this island, and of all the others that I have found all go naked, men and women, just as their mothers bring them forth. Of anything they have, if it be asked for, they never say no, but do rather invite the person to accept it, and show as much lovingness as though they would give their hearts. And whether it be a thing of value, or one of little worth, they are straightways content with whatsoever trifle of whatsoever kind may be given them in return for it. They are inclined to the love and service of their Highnesses and of all the Castilian nation, and they strive to combine in giving us things which they have in abundance, and of which we are in need. And they know no sect, or idolatry; save that they all believe that power and goodness are in the sky, and they believed very firmly that I, with these ships and crew, came from the sky; And this comes not because they are ignorant; on the contrary, they are men of very subtle wit, who navigate all those seas, and who give a marvelously good account of everything — but because they never saw men wearing clothes or the like of our ships. Christendom should give solemn thanks for the great exaltation they shall have by the conversion of so many peoples to our Holy faith; and next for the temporal benefit which will bring hither refreshment and profit, not only to Spain, but to all Christians. This briefly, in accordance with the facts. Dated, on the caravel, off the Canary Islands, the 15 February of the year 1493.

    At your command,

:Xpo FERENS./

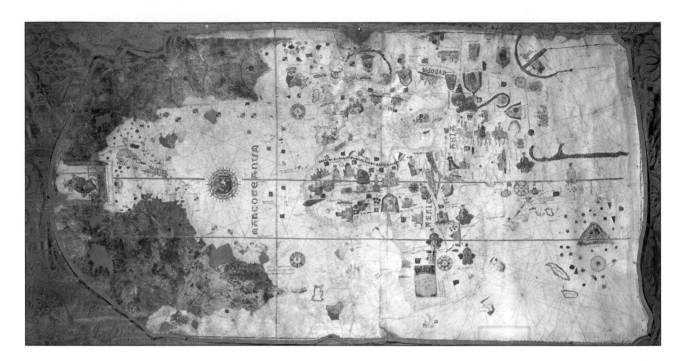

around the other islands in this group seeking the gold of "Cipangu." He found gold on the island of Hispaniola, and established a small colony.

Much of the letter extracted here, in which Columbus details his fabulous discovery, is taken up with the beauties of the landscape, the natural resources he found, and the peaceable character of the natives of the islands.

The natives' nakedness was as strange to 15th-century Europeans as the clothes worn by the newcomers were to the people of the islands. Mindful of the Spanish sovereign's interest in the treasures of "Cathay," Columbus emphasized that the people were ripe for conversion and exploitation; the natives seemed to regard Columbus and his men as heaven-sent kings, and their high regard for baubles suggested vast trading opportunities.

The *Santa María* went aground at Hispaniola and was lost, and Columbus sailed for home with the two caravels. He was delayed by storms at sea and arrived back in Palos on March 15, 1493. This letter was

Above: Map of the New World by Juan da Costa, who accompanied Columbus on his second voyage. At the far left, an image of Saint Christopher obscures a spot where Columbus expected to find a western passage.

enclosed with one written to Ferdinand and Isabella that has been lost. The letter was originally not addressed to any particular person, but was intended as a public announcement of Columbus's expedition and discoveries.

Ferdinand and Isabella had a number of manuscript copies of the letter made for their important officials, and one of these found its way to Luis de Santangel and Raphael Sanchez, treasury officials who had helped to raise funds for Columbus's expedition. The original Spanish version of the letter was quickly translated into Latin, partly to enable the pope to adjudicate Spanish and Portuguese claims to the New World.

The letter is dated February 15, 1493, "on the caravel off the Canaries," but historians have conjectured that in

European ships with Christian crosses on their sails arrive at a scene of cannibalism in this 1505 impression of "The people of the islands recently discovered."

fact Columbus wrote it within sight of the Azores on his return voyage. He clearly set out to arouse royal interest so that the king and queen would support a second voyage.

Columbus did not mention the track taken by his ships nor his dead reckoning computations of distance, in case the letter fell into the hands of enemies or rival navigators. He did not even mention the loss of his ship.

Comparison with Columbus's journal reveals the letter as a masterful, colorful précis of events,

Above: A 15th-century "round" ship, similar to the Santa María, *lies at anchor in Naples harbor.*

and the reply from Ferdinand and Isabella was all he could have hoped. Addressed to "Don Cristóbal Colón, Admiral of the Ocean Sea and Viceroy and Governor of the Islands that he has discovered in the Indies," their letter suggested he return to the New World immediately, offering to provide all necessary funds once he had presented himself at court.

HERNANDO PIZARRO
TO
THE OIDORES OF THE AUDIENCIA REAL OF SANTO DOMINGO

November 23, 1533

An excited conquistador gives the administrative council on Hispaniola an eyewitness account of the ambush and capture of the Inca king.

Hernando Pizarro, drawn two generations later by the Peruvian artist of mixed ancestry, Guaman Poma de Ayala.

An audiencia like the council at Santo Domingo on Hispaniola to which Hernando wrote.

 With astonishing violence, on November 16, 1532, a tiny force of Spanish conquistadores under Francisco Pizarro made a surprise attack on the Inca king, Atahualpa. This was the first move in Spain's conquest of Peru, in which the defenders' bows and arrows and slingstones were no match for heavily armored cavalry, and for the single-minded determination of the invaders.

On Pizarro's arrival in his lands, Atahualpa had himself offered the town of Cajamarca as a rest camp for the Spaniards—what had he to fear from a handful of men and their strange animals, these hitherto unheard-of horses? In response to Pizarro's invitation to a meeting in Cajamarca, he arrived in ceremonial state in his litter, a conveyance lined with macaws' feathers and adorned

Right: Gold mask from coastal Peru.

Left: Inca gold was not all metal. The wealth of Atahualpa rested on crops, especially the corn that his people grew.

with gold and silver. It was a further demonstration of his peaceful intentions that his company of several thousand warriors came armed only with small battle axes and slings. Hernando Pizarro's letter describes how the 62 Spanish horsemen and 106 soldiers waiting in Cajamarca were able to vanquish a force of thousands of Inca warriors in the town's main square, slaughtering two or three thousand of them. Trickery delivered the Indians' supreme ruler without any loss of Spanish blood.

The Pizarros were the most famous of the

Biography

Hernando Pizarro (1501–78) was the third brother of the more famous Francisco Pizarro, conqueror of Peru. The Pizarros were a family of adventurers from Trujillo in Spain (four of them took part in the Peruvian conquest). Hernando accompanied Francisco to Peru in 1531. In 1534 he was sent back to Spain to present the Spanish emperor, Charles, with a selection of Inca treasure. He returned to Peru and, as governor of Cuzco, became embroiled in the strife between rival factions of conquistadores. In 1538 he had an enemy executed. For this he was imprisoned for 21 years in Spain (1540–61), but he died immensely rich from the Inca gold he had plundered.

The Spaniards in armor and chain mail charged their horses straight into the mass of unarmed natives crowding the square. Trumpets were sounded and the Spanish troops gave their battle cry "Santiago!" They all placed rattles on their horses to terrify the Indians. With the booming of the shots and the trumpets and the troop of horses with their rattles, the Indians were thrown into confusion and panicked. The Spaniards fell upon them and began to kill. And as the Indians were unarmed they were routed without danger to any Christian.

The Governor armed himself with a quilted cotton coat of armor, drew his sword and dagger and entered the thick of the Indians with the Spaniards who were with him. With great bravery, he reached Atahualpa's litter. He fearlessly grabbed [the Inca's] left arm and shouted "Santiago," but he could not pull him out of his litter, which was on high. All those who were carrying Atahualpa's litter appeared to be important men, and they all died, as did those who were traveling in the litters and hammocks. They continued in this way for a long while, overpowering and killing the Indians until, becoming exhausted, one Spaniard stabbed [at the Inca] with his dagger to kill him. But Francisco Pizarro parried the blow, and from this parry the Spaniard, trying to strike Atahualpa, wounded the governor on the hand. Seven or eight [mounted] Spaniards spurred on and grabbed the edge of the litter, heaved on it and turned it onto its side. Atahualpa was captured in this way and the governor took him to his lodging. Those who were carrying the litter and those who escorted [the Inca] never abandoned him: all died around him.

In the space of two hours . . . all those troops were annihilated. That day, six or seven thousand Indians lay dead on the plain and many more had their arms cut off. . . . Atahualpa himself admitted that we had killed seven thousand of his Indians in that battle. It was an extraordinary thing to see so great a ruler captured in so short a time, when he had come with such might.

PIZARRO

19

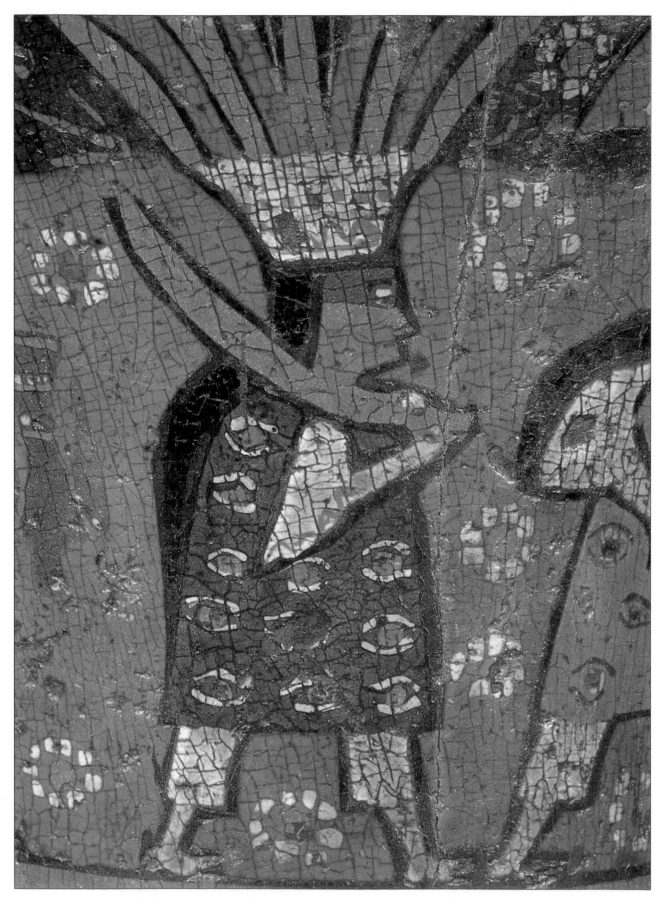

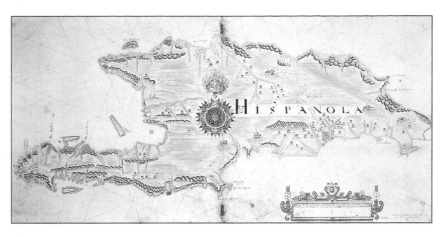

conquistador families. Francisco (about 1478–1541) served under Balboa, the first European to see the Pacific (1513). Francisco and his friend Diego de Almagro became free-lance adventurers in the 1520's and learned of the wealth of the Inca empire. Determined to emulate the feats of Cortés, the conqueror of Mexico, Francisco returned to Spain in 1529 to obtain royal sanction for the conquest of Peru. Charles V appointed him captain-general, with Almagro as commandant of Tumbes. Pizarro sailed from Panama in December 1531 with just 183 men, landed at Tumbes on the Peruvian coast in May 1532, and began the journey inland. With Pizarro were other members of his family: his brothers Juan (killed during the Inca siege of Cuzco in 1536), Hernando (1501–1578), and Gonzalo.

The Pizarros proved to be cruel and treacherous, repeatedly breaking their promises and pledges of safe conduct to the Incas. After promising Atahualpa his freedom in return for an enormous ransom of pure gold, Francisco accepted the gold, then executed the king in July 1533.

The Incas were not alone in suffering at the hands of the Pizarros. After taking Cuzco, the Inca capital known as the City of the Sun, and setting up a puppet ruler, Francisco left to found Lima and other cities, while his friend Diego de Almagro undertook the conquest of Chile. An Inca insurrection in 1536 led to a siege of Cuzco that was thwarted only when Almagro returned from Chile. Almagro had found no wealth in Chile and hoped to oust his old friend, Francisco Pizarro. Francisco sent his brother Hernando against Almagro. Hernando had him beheaded, an act that would have two profound consequences—Almagro's followers assassinated Francisco Pizarro, and Hernando was recalled to

Spain in disgrace for exceeding his authority. He was imprisoned for 20 years. The last of the Pizarro brood, Gonzalo (about 1506–48), rebelled against Spain's viceroy to Peru, sent out in 1544, and defeated and killed him in battle. The next emissary from Spain gathered a powerful army; Gonzalo was defeated and beheaded.

The conquest of Peru occurred in a pivotal period of Indian history. Unlike Cortés, who had encountered the Aztecs of Mexico at the height of their power, the Pizarros collided with an empire in the ascendant—the Incas had first extended their sway over Peru as recently as 1440. The Pizarros enjoyed incredible luck, entering Peru when a bloody civil war was raging over the succession to the Inca throne. Atahualpa had only just won the war when he had his encounter with Pizarro. Had the conquistadores landed a few years earlier or later, they might have found the Incas' military power intact.

Left: A warrior in feather headdress, holding a spear, painted on a wooden Inca vase.

Above: A 1633 map of Hispaniola, Caribbean seat of the judicial council to which Hernando addressed his letter.

Right: The conquistadores' "kettle helmets," mostly made in Germany, echoed an ancient Greek military style.

GALILEO GALILEI
TO
BELISARIO VINTA

January 7, 1610

*Galileo describes hitherto unknown
details about the moon, now visible through his
powerful astronomical telescope.*

*Galileo Galilei: the heavens he
observed did not match the
heavens his times believed in.*

When Galileo proved that all falling bodies, great or small, descend with equal velocity, he simultaneously disproved Aristotle's long-established assumption that a heavier body always falls faster. At the time, Galileo was a mathematics lecturer at the University of Pisa in Italy. His remarkable discovery would bring him fame, but not before the hostility of the faction that supported the ideas of Aristotle had forced him to leave the university. Galileo then became professor of mathematics at Padua. His perfection while there of a recent Dutch invention—the telescope—would make him a figure of world renown and ultimately bring him into conflict with the church. Galileo built and improved his own telescope, applying his mathematical genius to the problems of refraction (the deflection of light passing through glass), and grinding and polishing Venetian glass for his lenses. He demonstrated the apparatus to his patron, the doge of Venice, from the bell tower of St. Mark's in Venice, impressing him with the view of Padua, 24 miles away. Not yet satisfied, Galileo produced telescopes that magnified 20 and 30 times.

Turning his technically assisted eye on the heavens, he observed that the earth seemed not to be stationary at the center of the planetary system, as in the currently accepted model of the universe. He was convinced that the Polish astronomer, Nicholas Copernicus (1473–1543), had been correct in suggesting in 1543 that the sun, not the earth, was at the center of this system of planets.

*Below: Galileo's personal
astrolabe, an early instrument
for measuring latitude.*

Biography

Galileo Galilei (1564–1642) began his academic career as a student of medicine at the university in his native Pisa, studying mathematics privately. While watching a lamp swing from the ceiling of a cathedral he inferred that a pendulum's swings are equal in time whatever their range. This principle would later be applied to clocks. A lecturer in Pisa by 1589, he became professor of mathematics at Padua in 1592. He applied mathematics to the analysis of objects in motion, laying a basis on which Sir Isaac Newton was later to build his comprehensive physics. Galileo was also a talented painter, played the flute, and read widely in the classics.

To satisfy you I shall briefly recount what I have observed with one of my telescopes looking at the face of the Moon, which I have been able to see very near; I having employed a telescope that represents it of diameter twenty times that which appears to the naked eye, whence the surface is seen 400 times and the volume 8000 times that which it ordinarily displays. What is there can be discerned with great distinctness, and in fact it is seen that the Moon is most evidently not at all of an even, smooth and regular surface, as a great many people believe of it and of the other heavenly bodies, but on the contrary it is rough and unequal. It is full of prominences and cavities similar, but much larger, to the mountains and valleys spread over the Earth's surface. The boundary between the lighted part and the rest of the dark body is seen to be not part of an oval line sharply marked, but a very confused boundary, rough and broken. Near this are seen various luminous points situated in the dark part and completely separated from the lighted horn, which points gradually go growing and enlarging so that after some hours they unite with the luminous part.

There are further seen in the lighted part a great many small dark spots bounded by certain luminous (partial) rims which all face toward the side from which the light of the Sun is coming. I have observed many other details, and I hope to observe still more of them. We may believe that we have been the first in the world to discover anything of the celestial bodies from so near, and so distinctly.

Galileo Galilei.

Galileo went on to chart the movement of the planets in relation to the sun. He studied the moon and described his detailed observations in the letter to a colleague abstracted here. He declared the Milky Way to be a collection of countless stars and inferred the rotation of the sun. He also discovered four of Jupiter's satellites.

Unfortunately, Galileo's discoveries coincided with a period of repression in the church. The church's leaders feared any free thinking, especially relating to the interpretation of the scriptures. In 1616 Galileo bowed to church pressure,

Right: Moon sketches by Galileo and two sections of his telescope.

promising to abstain from all future advocacy of "heretical" doctrines. By 1632, he judged it safe to publish a major work on cosmology. However, he was summoned before the Inquisition, the book was banned, and he was sentenced to imprisonment. This sentence was commuted and he spent the last years of his life under house arrest.

SAMUEL PEPYS
TO
LADY ELIZABETH CARTERET

September 4, 1665

*The English diarist and civil servant
describes the horrors of bubonic plague in a
crowded city.*

*Samuel Pepys, best remembered
for his diary, deciphered from
code and published in 1825.*

*A London
street crier of
1666, selling
his wares.*

When Pepys wrote the letter abstracted here, London was in the grip of the plague. England had suffered severe outbreaks of plague before, in 1603, 1625, and from 1640 to 1647, during the English Civil War. The Great Plague of 1664–65 carried off more than 70,000 people. It began its peak in April, and was exacerbated by a long, hot, dry summer. On April 30 Pepys began reporting deaths from "the sickness" in his diary, and on June 7 he recorded sighting a house marked with the large red crosses that warned of plague within.

With primitive sanitation and no real medical knowledge, London's defenses were perfunctory: some of the so-called "plague nurses" were old women who robbed the dead and dying; victims were shut up inside their houses; huge pits were dug for mass burial, while the bodies of those who died on the streets lay stinking where they fell. Shops and theaters closed, and the royal court and officialdom decamped to the country.

Pepys was well aware of the danger. By mid-June he had sent his wife, his mother, and the maids out of town. However, he stayed on in London, not only braving death and working hard, but also philandering and in other ways enjoying himself as was his custom. His courage was rewarded: he survived and prospered.

Lady Elizabeth Carteret (c. 1610–80) was the wife of Sir George, navy treasurer and Pepys's influential

*London Bridge as it appeared
in Pepys's day, with houses
built along it.*

Now that by the dispatch of the fleet I am at liberty to retire wholly to Woolwich, your Ladyship shall find no further cause to reproach me my silence, I having stayed in the city till above 7,400 died in one week, and of them above 6,000 of the plague, and little noise heard day nor night but tolling of bells; till I could walk Lumber street and not meet twenty persons from one end to the other, and not fifty upon the Exchange; till whole families (ten and twelve together) have been swept away; till my very physician, Dr. Burnet, who undertook to secure me against any infection (having survived the month of his own being shut up) died himself of the plague; till the nights (though much lengthened) are grown too short to conceal the burials of those that died the day before, people being thereby constrained to borrow daylight for that service; lastly, till I could find neither meat nor drink safe, the butcheries being everywhere visited, my brewer's house shut up, and my baker with his whole family dead of the plague. Yet, Madam, through God's blessing and the good humors begot in my attendance upon our late Amours, your poor servant is in a perfect state of health, as well as resolution of employing it as your Ladyship and family shall find work for it. I'll go no further in this disagreeable discourse, hoping my next may bring you a more welcome account of the lessening of the disease; which God say Amen to.

Pepys

Top: Spectacles that Pepys had specially made to shield his eyes from direct light.

Left: A corpse-collector's bell, vials for remedies, the record of London deaths for September 19–26, 1665, a 1666 spoon commemorating the plague, and a jar for burning medicinal herbs.

colleague. Earlier that summer Pepys's patron and relative, the Earl of Sandwich, had given a boost to Pepys's prestige by using him as a go-between in arranging a marriage between the earl's daughter and the Carterets' son.

Pepys performed the task to the great satisfaction of both families. The "late amours" he mentions in the letter are a reference to the wedding, which, according to his diary, he had attended on July 31.

BENJAMIN FRANKLIN
TO
JOSEPH BANKS

December 1, 1783

The American statesman and scientist writes an enthusiastic report to his botanist friend after the first manned ascent in a hydrogen balloon.

Benjamin Franklin, who predicted that balloons would eliminate warfare.

Sir Joseph Banks, explorer, naturalist, and president of the Royal Society.

The correspondence between Benjamin Franklin and Sir Joseph Banks—both products of the 18th-century Enlightenment—was a true meeting of minds. A successful self-taught businessman and a major political figure, Franklin began at the age of 40 the research into electricity that would win him fellowship of the Royal Society—the premier British body for the advancement of science. He explained the difference between positive and negative electricity, showed that lightning is caused by electricity, and invented the lightning rod. He discovered the path of storms over North America, the course of the Gulf Stream, and the reason for the Gulf Stream's high temperature. He also investigated the powers of various colors to absorb solar heat, and invented bifocal glasses.

Sir Joseph Banks (1743–1820), best known as a botanist, first came to prominence in 1768–71, when in a vessel equipped at his own expense he directed botanical investigations during Captain Cook's round-the-world expedition. Banks also made field trips to Newfoundland (1766) and to the Hebrides (1772), and in 1778 was elected president of the Royal Society, a post he held for 41 years.

As a diplomat living in Paris, Franklin followed with keen interest the development of balloon flight. Some observers regarded balloons as little more than extraordinary toys, but with characteristic perceptiveness Franklin realized the significance of manned

---

Biography

Benjamin Franklin (1706–90) was born in Boston, Massachusetts, the youngest son and 10th child of a family of 17. After an early apprenticeship in printing he became, first, a prominent journalist, and then a noted scientist. He was instrumental in establishing public services: a fire department, a lending library, an insurance company, and the academy that became the University of Pennsylvania. In 1776 he helped to draft the Declaration of Independence. A skilled diplomat, he negotiated both the U.S. treaty with France in 1778 and British recognition of the United States in 1783. He was American minister in Paris until 1785, and he helped to frame the American Constitution of 1787.

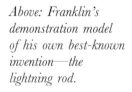

Above: Franklin's demonstration model of his own best-known invention—the lightning rod.

Right: A plate commemorating a balloon flight by the Robert brothers in 1784.

In mine of yesterday, I promis'd to give you an Account of Messrs. Charles and Robert's Experiment. About One o'Clock, the Air became tolerably clear, to the great Satisfaction of the Spectators, who were infinite, Notice having been given of the intended Experiment several Days before in the Papers. Never before was a philosophical Experiment so magnificently attended. Some Guns were fired to give Notice, that the Departure of the great Balloon was near. Means were used, I am told, to prevent the great Balloon's rising so high as might endanger its Bursting. Several Bags of Sand were taken on board before the Cord that held it down was cut; and the whole Weight being then too much to be lifted, such a Quantity was discharg'd as to permit its Rising slowly.

All Eyes were gratified with seeing it rise majestically from among the Trees, and ascend gradually above the Buildings, a most beautiful Spectacle! The brave Adventurers held out and wav'd a little white Pennant, on both sides of their Car, to salute the Spectators, who return'd loud Claps of Applause. The Wind was very little, so that the Object, tho' moving to the Northward, continued long in View; and it was a great while before the admiring People began to disperse.

The Persons embark'd were Mr. Charles and One of the Messieurs Robert, the very ingenious Constructors of the Machine. I had a Pocket Glass, with which I follow'd it, till I lost Sight, first of the Men, then of the Car, and when I last saw the Balloon, it appear'd no bigger than a Walnut. What became of them is not yet known here. I hope they descended by Daylight, so as to see and avoid falling among Trees or on Houses, and that the Experiment was completed without any mischievous Accident.

Tuesday Morning, December 2.
I am reliev'd from my Anxiety, by hearing that the Adventurers descended well near l'Isle Adam, before Sunset. If I receive any farther Particulars of Importance, I shall communicate them hereafter.

27

flight. In July 1783 he wrote to Banks: "I begin to be almost sorry I was born so soon, since I cannot have the happiness of knowing what will be known one hundred years hence."

The pioneers in aeronautical invention were the Montgolfier brothers, Joseph Michel (1740–1810) and Jacques Étienne (1745–99). In 1783 they launched their first, unmanned, hot-air balloon. Later in the summer of 1783 a balloon went aloft for an eight-minute flight with three passengers inside its basket: a rooster, a duck, and a sheep. They returned safely, and the next stage was a manned flight. Who would make this dangerous first step? Louis XVI, who had been following the Montgolfiers' experiments, suggested that condemned men be used.

Professor Jacques Alexandre Charles (1746–1823), whose unmanned hydrogen balloon had already achieved an altitude of 3,000 feet, proposed himself. However, he was pipped at the post by Pilâtre du Rozier and the Marquis d'Arlandes, who flew across Paris in a hot-air balloon for 25 minutes at 300 feet on November 21, 1783. In the letter extracted here, Franklin recounts Charles's flight in December, with the younger of the two Robert brothers, the engineers who made his balloon. Charles made a second ascent alone that evening and became the first person to see a sunset twice in one day.

In the decade of balloon mania, the 1780's, Franklin became certain that balloons would convince "sovereigns of the folly of wars . . . since it will be impracticable for the most potent of them to guard his dominions." History would prove him far too optimistic.

Balloons were used by Napoleon for reconnaissance, and during the American Civil War the North used large yellow balloons to spy on Confederate lines before the battle of Richmond, forcing the South to develop a rifled antiaircraft gun in response. During the Prussian siege of Paris in 1870, the balloon really came into its own. In all, 65 balloons left Paris during the siege; 45 reached the French lines safely, carrying 164 passengers, 381 pigeons, 5 dogs, 2.5 million letters, and 11 tons of official dispatches.

Balloons convinced no one "of the folly of wars," but balloon technology is still being developed more than 200 years later. A cheap way of reaching the upper atmosphere, balloons are used in telecommunications and atmospheric research.

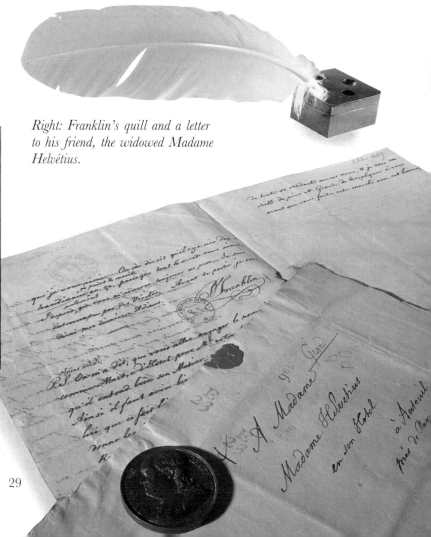

Right: Franklin's quill and a letter to his friend, the widowed Madame Helvétius.

Above: An 1803 French cartoon, fancifully picturing new technologies in a French invasion of England.

Left: A 1780's artist's impression of how du Rozier's flight must have looked from Franklin's balcony.

THE COMTE DE BOUGAINVILLE
TO
THE MINISTER OF THE MARINE

April, 1768

*The accomplished French navigator
reports on the open and unabashed attitude
of Tahitian women to sexuality.*

*Louis Antoine, comte de
Bougainville, drawn by the
expedition's artist.*

he first European to land on the beautiful South Pacific island of Tahiti was Capt. Samuel Wallis, who reached the island on June 19, 1767, in a British ship, the *Dolphin*. Wallis was struck by Tahitian manners. The people were of volatile temper and were also great thieves. Wallis had eventually to turn his ship's guns on the Polynesian outriggers to stop their pilfering. Most startling however, was the Tahitians' practice of free love. Women would, with their men's consent, trade their favors with the sex-starved sailors for nails and other prized pieces of ironwork. All these findings were confirmed by Tahiti's second European visitor, who made a more extensive study of the island.

On April 6, 1768, Capt. Louis

*Above: Tahiti, a romantic view
of the island by William Hodges
(1744–97), ship's artist with
Capt. Cook in 1773.*

Antoine de Bougainville reached Tahiti in his two ships, the *Boudeuse* and the *Étoile*. He traveled officially for the French government, charged with making the first French circumnavigation of the globe. Bougainville described Tahiti in his journal as the "New Cythera"—in Greek mythology Cythera was the island of Aphrodite, goddess of love. Later he made the account official in a letter to the French minister of the marine.

The physical beauty of Tahiti, with its mountains, forests, and sparkling lagoons, increased the Frenchman's sense of having been transported to the Garden of Eden. Bougainville spent 10 days

---

Biography

Louis Antoine de Bougainville (1729–1811) was born in Paris. He served with distinction as a soldier during the Seven Years War and then joined the navy in 1763. He made rapid strides, commanding the first French circumnavigation of the world (1766–69), and writing an influential account of his travels, *Description of a Voyage Around the World* (1771–72). He commanded several ships of the line, and achieved a unique double distinction: *chef d'escadre* (commodore) in the navy and field marshal in the army. After the outbreak of the French Revolution, he devoted himself to scientific pursuits. Napoleon made him a senator, count of the empire, and member of the Légion d'Honneur.

They pressed us to choose a woman and come ashore with her; and their gestures, which were nothing less than equivocal, denoted in what manner we should form an acquaintance with her. It was very difficult in such conditions, to keep at their work four hundred French sailors who had not seen a woman for six months. In spite of all our precautions a young girl came on board and placed herself upon the quarter-deck near one of the hatchways, which was open in order to give air to those who were heaving at the capstan below it. The girl carelessly dropped a cloth which covered her, and appeared to the eyes of all beholders such as Venus showed herself to the Phrygian shepherd, having indeed the celestial form of that goddess. Both sailors and soldiers endeavored to come to the hatchway, and the capstan was never hove with more alacrity than on this occasion.

The sailors were invited to enter the houses where the people gave them to eat; nor did the civility of their landlords stop at a slight collation: they offered them young girls. The hut was immediately filled with a curious crowd of men and women who made a circle round the guest and the young victim of hospitality. The ground was spread with leaves and flowers, and their musicians sang a hymeneal song to the tune of their flutes. Here Venus is goddess of hospitality, her worship does not admit of any mysteries and every tribute paid to her is a feast for the whole nation. They were surprised at the confusion which our people appeared to be in as our customs do not allow of these public proceedings. However, I would not answer for it that every one of our men found it impossible to conquer his repugnance and conform to the customs of the country.

BOUGAINVILLE

in Tahiti, filling casks with fresh water, cutting wood, and nursing 34 scurvy-stricken sailors back to health with the precious vitamin C from the island's abundant fruit. Like Wallis, he was constantly plagued by theft, for the Tahitians' attitudes toward property differed as greatly from the Europeans' as did their sexual practices.

Sex most engaged Bougainville's interest and that of other French diarists and letter writers, who discovered that unmarried girls could take partners whenever they wished; married women enjoyed an almost equal liberty.

The 400 lusty sailors from Bougainville's ships were overjoyed to find sex available for the price of a few nails. The reality had its hidden cost, though: the islanders expected a man to copulate with a woman in front of an audience. Each sexual act attracted up to 50 onlookers.

The Frenchmen must have adjusted. They were soon prized as lovers by Tahitian women, but Bougainville forbade his officers to take part in the general lovemaking. Fear of syphilis, already a scourge on the island, may have contributed to his decision, but more important was his concern that his officers could not maintain discipline on the voyage home if men under them had watched them coupling in public.

The *Boudeuse* and the *Étoile* left Tahiti on April 15 and completed their round-the-world tour, arriving at St. Malo in March 1769 after two years and four months. Bougainville's reports about Tahiti created a sensation, and seemed to confirm the "noble savage" theory of the French philosopher Jean Jacques Rousseau, who believed that the ills of civilization could be cured if humans could return to their primitive state.

Rousseau had first expounded his idealized concept in the

Bougainvillea spectabilis, *a shrub bearing the count's name, is native to South America. A strait and a tropical island were also named after him.*

Discourse on the Origin of the Inequality of Man (published in 1755), and later in *The Social Contract* (1762). The noble savage, wrote Rousseau, had no houses or property, and the sexes "united without design, as accident, opportunity, or inclination brought them together."

Rousseau's noble savages wore no clothes, built no houses, fenced no fields, sowed no seeds, and did not form into families, tribes, or nations; they enjoyed perfect freedom and absolute equality. Rousseau argued that inequality came about because humans passed from the innocence of the primitive life to the corruption of society. His message of liberty, equality, and fraternity would become a rallying cry in the French Revolution.

Bougainville rebutted Rousseau's idea that primitive man was superior to the civilized variety, and also greatly resented his statement that soldiers, sailors, and merchants could not be trusted to convey the real, inner truth about the Pacific Islands. He was at pains to point out that Tahiti was no utopia—free love and the bounties of nature had their dark side in slavery, bondage, human sacrifice, and intellectual apathy.

Bougainville also criticized Abbé Prévost, author of the 18th-century bestseller *Manon Lescaut*, for popularizing a romantic style in travel writing that left out all the solid scientific data that was of inestimable value to navigators and mariners. Bougainville was a man of the Enlightenment in terms of his scientific approach to discovery and navigation; in terms of searching for new social ideals, he was not.

Left: Ideas for better chronometers (timekeepers for determining longitude, such as this 1759 model by Harrison), not for utopias, preoccupied the navigator Bougainville.

Right: Woman With Mango, *by Paul Gauguin whose views of Tahiti and its people, 100 years later, closely resembled those of Rousseau.*

QIANLONG, EMPEROR OF CHINA
TO
GEORGE III, KING OF ENGLAND

October 3, 1793

*China's emperor accepts Britain's "tribute"
while rejecting George III's requests for trading concessions and
closer diplomatic and cultural links.*

Qianlong, who invited the British monarch to secure peace and prosperity through perpetual submission.

George III, whose less populous and more unruly empire was the more powerful.

n September 21, 1792, three British warships left Spithead in Hampshire for a voyage to China. Commanding the expedition was Lord Macartney (1737–1806), a career diplomat who had seen service in Russia, Ireland, Grenada, and India. Macartney's instructions from Henry Dundas, the British home secretary, were to establish trading links with China and to secure a permanent British embassy in Beijing. At this time there were no diplomatic contacts between Europe and China, and the British hoped to steal a march on their trading rivals, the Dutch and the French. Macartney's expedition reached China in May

---

Biography

Qianlong (1711–99), fourth of the Ch'ing (Manchu) emperors, reigned from 1735 until 1796. He was a successful military leader, who strengthened Chinese authority by enlarging the empire and quelling challenges from Tibet, Nepal, Burma, and Annam. Qianlong was also a scholar, and he practiced the arts of painting and calligraphy as well as writing poetry. He sponsored a 10-year project aimed at compiling a comprehensive collection of classic Chinese works of literature and learning. However, the cost of his military campaigns depleted the country's finances, and the last 20 years of his reign were marred by poor management and corruption.

1793, though not until the morning of September 14 did he finally come face to face with the 82-year-old emperor, Qianlong. Three weeks later the emperor sent the official answer extracted here to Macartney for transmission to George III, thus signaling the failure of the British mission. The letter stands as the most important document of Chinese–Western relations in the 700 years between Marco Polo and Deng Xiaoping.

The British thought of themselves as one equal power dealing with another. Qianlong, the Celestial One, ruler of the Middle Empire with a population of 300 million against Britain's eight million, not only despised these white men as "barbarians" but also held an implacable view of them as vassals, just as he saw emissaries from any other

Right: The Chinese imperial dragon motif, from a silk robe of the 1700's.

Far right: The letter to George III, in Manchu (left), in Latin (center), and (right) in Mandarin.

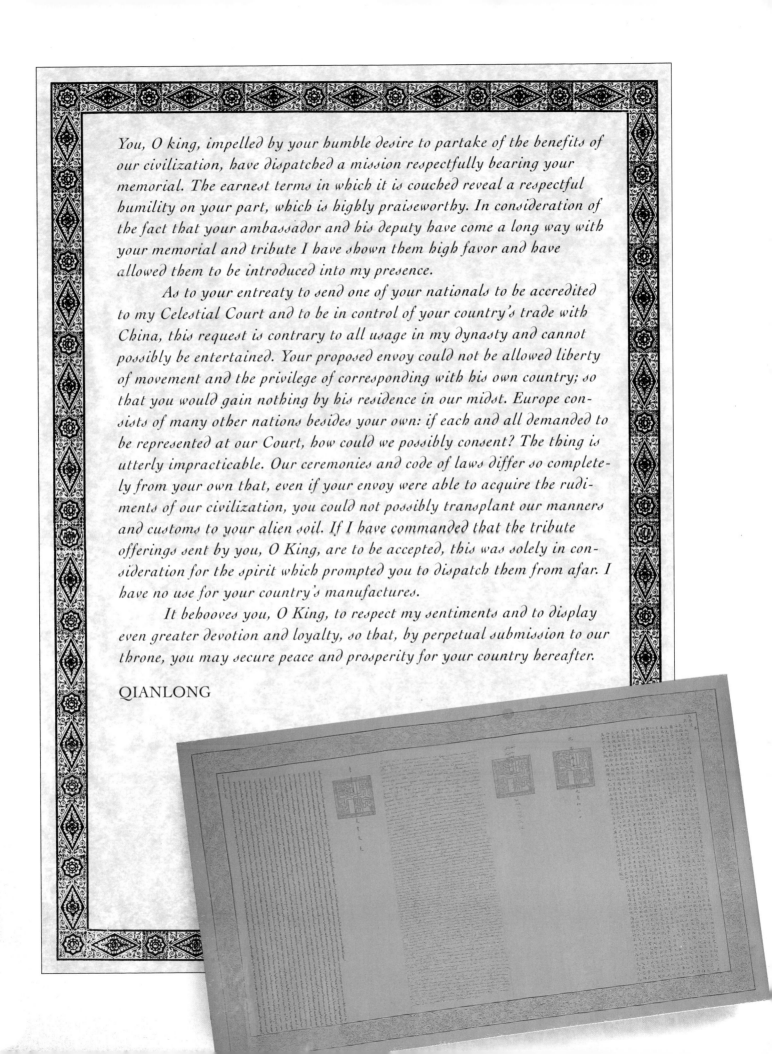

You, O king, impelled by your humble desire to partake of the benefits of our civilization, have dispatched a mission respectfully bearing your memorial. The earnest terms in which it is couched reveal a respectful humility on your part, which is highly praiseworthy. In consideration of the fact that your ambassador and his deputy have come a long way with your memorial and tribute I have shown them high favor and have allowed them to be introduced into my presence.

As to your entreaty to send one of your nationals to be accredited to my Celestial Court and to be in control of your country's trade with China, this request is contrary to all usage in my dynasty and cannot possibly be entertained. Your proposed envoy could not be allowed liberty of movement and the privilege of corresponding with his own country; so that you would gain nothing by his residence in our midst. Europe consists of many other nations besides your own: if each and all demanded to be represented at our Court, how could we possibly consent? The thing is utterly impracticable. Our ceremonies and code of laws differ so completely from your own that, even if your envoy were able to acquire the rudiments of our civilization, you could not possibly transplant our manners and customs to your alien soil. If I have commanded that the tribute offerings sent by you, O King, are to be accepted, this was solely in consideration for the spirit which prompted you to dispatch them from afar. I have no use for your country's manufactures.

It behooves you, O King, to respect my sentiments and to display even greater devotion and loyalty, so that, by perpetual submission to our throne, you may secure peace and prosperity for your country hereafter.

QIANLONG

tribe and country. This collision of attitudes had shown itself in the conflict over Macartney's refusal to kowtow—the ritual that was normally performed by officials and foreign representatives granted an audience with the Chinese emperor.

From a standing position a vassal would kneel on both knees, bend until his head touched the ground, raise his torso, and then bow again until his forehead touched the ground a second time, then a third. He would then have to stand upright and repeat the sequence twice more.

Macartney refused to observe this "degrading" ritual. He pointed out that no ambassador could ever do greater honor to a foreign prince than to his own king, and that in London he was required simply to go down on one knee and kiss the monarch's hand; he would bend both knees only to God. Qianlong's advisers recoiled in horror at the very thought of a barbarian touching their emperor. In the event Macartney went down on one knee three times, and politely bowed his head.

The tone of Qianlong's letter, only part of which appears here, demonstrates that he did not accept the English king as an equal. Despite Macartney's insistence that the British were not vassals, Qianlong's original letter, written in Mandarin, was considered so haughty and condescending that it was toned down, first by the missionaries who translated it into Latin and then by Macartney when he summarized it in English.

Even if Macartney had kowtowed, it is unlikely that Qianlong would have granted his requests. Chinese civilization, which had survived for thousands of years, was static, changeless, and self-sufficient. The emperor wanted it to continue

Left: Imperial dragons writhe up and down the cover of a book of calligraphy by Qianlong.

that way. In addition, Chinese society was xenophobic: Westerners earned the sobriquet "foreign devils" because they wore trousers—in China, only pantomime demons in the theater were ever seen thus attired.

Moreover, 1793 was a particularly inauspicious year for a European to seek a permanent legation in China, for this was the year of the Terror in France, when the Revolution reached new heights of bloodshed. Reports had reached Qianlong of the French revolutionaries' determination to impose universal brotherhood on the entire world, at gunpoint if necessary.

In light of such news, the superior military technology of the "foreign devils"—evident from the most cursory examination of the British warships as they lay at anchor in Tianjin harbor—was all the more disturbing. For a short time Qianlong even considered having holes drilled in the ships below the waterline, using local pearlfishers as frogmen. It is the symbolism in this collision of cultures in 1793 that has so fascinated

Above: Kirghizian emissaries from Central Asia offer gifts to Qianlong in the manner to which he was accustomed.

Left: A week before Macartney set sail, the cartoonist James Gillray published this impression of what Macartney's meeting with the emperor would be like.

historians, who see in it a classic case of opposing ways of life: tradition versus modernity, the agricultural society versus the industrial, the closed society against the open, the Asian mode of production against capitalism; in modern terms, East versus West.

Despite their hostility to the West, the Chinese allowed the envoy to travel overland from Beijing back to Guangzhou. Macartney was thus able to fulfill the second aim of his mission and learn about techniques of silk and tea production in China. He took the secrets back to Bengal, where the British East India Company at once set up production in direct competition to the Chinese.

Unlike Peter the Great in Russia in the late 17th century, and the Meiji dynasty in Japan after 1868, Qianlong turned his back on the West. The British sent another mission to China in 1816, which was also rebuffed. The consequences of China's unshakably traditional perspective and isolationism would begin to be seen in the 1840's, when British military might was to humiliate China in the first Opium War.

COMMODORE M. C. PERRY
TO
HIS IMPERIAL MAJESTY, THE EMPEROR OF JAPAN

July 7, 1853

*On behalf of President Fillmore, Perry
asks Japan to enter into friendly relations
with the United States.*

*Commodore Matthew Perry,
who opened the way for trade
with Japan.*

fter the Portuguese, under the explorer Vasco da Gama, reached India in 1498, their expansion into the Far East was rapid. In their wake came the new order of Catholic missionaries, the Jesuits, led by Saint Francis Xavier, who made a remarkable number of converts to their faith, while at the same time arousing the animosity of powerful Japanese. As the Japanese learned more about European activity in other regions, they became increasingly alarmed. Once Christianity gained a foothold, military conquest seemed to follow. Beginning in 1597, the rulers of Japan persecuted Japanese Christians, who finally rebelled in 1638. Japanese rulers proceeded to wipe out Christian converts and to expel all foreigners. For 200 years Japan remained almost completely isolated, maintaining contact only through a tiny Dutch and Chinese trading station at Nagasaki.

The force that prised open Japan came from an unexpected direction—the east—for in 1852 President Millard Fillmore sent a squadron of four ships under Commodore Matthew Perry to prepare the way for trading concessions. The United States government's interest in Japan was partly prompted by the steamship, which meant that ships could now sail from California to Japan in 18 days. In addition, the California gold rush, which yielded $60 million a year in the early 1850's, had created sizable funds for investment in international trade. The United States wanted to make Japan a focus for trade and investment, in keeping with 19th-century U.S. policy to acquire the economic advantages of empire without incurring the kind of military and administrative costs the British had endured in India. The government also wanted to protect the crews of its whaling fleets. Whaling was big

A champion wrestler trounces a Western sailor in a Japanese caricature from 1861.

The undersigned, commander-in-chief of all the naval forces of the United States of America stationed in the East India, China and Japan seas, has been sent by his government to this country, on a friendly mission, with ample powers to negotiate with the government of Japan, touching certain matters which have been fully set forth in the letter of the President of the United States, copies of which, together with copies of the letter of credence of the undersigned, in the English, Dutch, and Chinese languages, are herewith transmitted.

The undersigned has been commanded to state that the President entertains the most friendly feelings toward Japan, but has been surprised and grieved to learn that when any of the people of the United States go, of their own accord, or are thrown by the perils of the sea, within the dominions of your imperial majesty, they are treated as if they were your worst enemies.

With the Americans, as indeed with all Christian people, it is considered a sacred duty to receive with kindness, and to succor and protect all, of whatever nation, who may be cast upon their shores, and such has been the course of the Americans with respect to all Japanese subjects who have fallen under their protection.

The government of the United States desires to obtain from that of Japan some positive assurance that persons who may hereafter be shipwrecked on the coast of Japan, or driven by stress of weather into her ports, shall be treated with humanity . . . they inhabit a great country which lies directly between Japan and Europe . . . we now have large cities, from which, with the aid of steam-vessels, we can reach Japan in eighteen or twenty days; that our commerce with all this region of the globe is rapidly increasing, and the Japan seas will soon be covered with our vessels. . . . The undersigned hold out all these arguments in the hope that the Japanese government will see the necessity of averting unfriendly collision between the two nations, by responding favorably to the propositions of amity, which are now made in all sincerity.

Many of the large ships-of-war destined to visit Japan have not yet arrived in these seas, though they are hourly expected; and the undersigned, as an evidence of his friendly intentions, has brought but four of the smaller ones, designing, should it become necessary, to return to Yedo in the ensuing spring with a much larger force.

With the most profound respect for your imperial majesty, and entertaining a sincere hope that you may long live to enjoy health and happiness, the undersigned subscribes himself.

M C Perry.

business in the 1850's, and the fleets from Nantucket, New Bedford, and other eastern ports followed a worldwide track in pursuit of the sperm whale that took them close to the stormy and hazardous coasts of Japan.

On July 8, 1853, Commodore Perry sailed his squadron of four ships into Uraga, Edo Bay. He brought a letter from President Fillmore that stressed America's desire for peaceful relations with Japan, and mentioned only the issues of humane treatment for ship-wrecked whaling

crews, facilities for coaling and revictualing of American ships in Japanese ports, and some vague proposals on trade. However, Perry's own letter strongly hinted that refusal of these requests could lead to war, and he warned that he would return in the spring of 1854 with a larger squadron and would expect a satisfactory answer.

Japan's rulers realized that their country would be unable to resist Western warships. They particularly feared that war with the United States might well be the signal for even more powerful predators, such as the British, to move in and dismember their island nation. There were

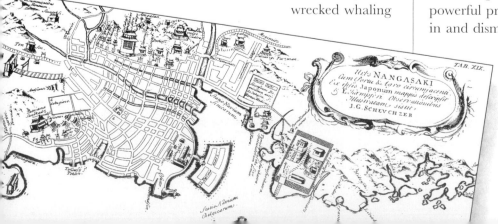

Above: Woodblock print of the model railway Perry presented to Japan.

Left: Part of an early map of Nagasaki.

Top right: Inro Japanese lacquered box.

Some of Perry's gifts to the Japanese

For the emperor:
Five rifles
Three muskets
12 cavalry swords
20 army pistols
A box of books
A box of perfumery
A barrel of whiskey
A cask of wine
A telescope
Cherry cordials
Champagne

For distribution to important persons:
Pistols, rifles, carbines, ammunition
11 cavalry swords
Four volumes of Audubon's *Birds of America*
Three volumes of Audubon's *Quadrupeds*
A box of China ware
Two telegraph instruments
Three lifeboats
Up-to-date charts of the world's coastal waters
Tea
Several clocks
100 gallons of whiskey
Eight baskets of Irish potatoes
Standard United States balances
Agricultural implements

Some of the Japanese gifts to the Americans

From the emperor:
A gold-lacquered paper box
A gold-lacquered bookcase
A lacquered writing table
A bronze incense-burner
A silver flower holder
20 pieces of fine silk
10 pieces of crepe
Two braziers
300 chickens
200 bundles of rice

From the officials of the emperor:
11 pieces of crepe
36 pieces of fine silk
30 coir-fiber brooms
Four boxes of seashells
35 bundles of oak charcoal
Five boxes of stamped note and letter paper
Woven bamboo articles
20 Japanese umbrellas
A lacquered paper box
10 jars of soy sauce
Eight boxes of dolls
Flowered note paper
30 sets of lacquered cups
Several porcelain goblets

divided counsels among the members of Japan's ruling shogunate. A few of them advocated resistance to the West at any cost. The majority, however, took the view that in such a war defeat was inevitable, and that the best course was to engage for a time in trade with the West, using the profits to build up viable military forces of their own, equipped with modern firepower.

When Perry returned in February 1854 with eight warships, the shogunate therefore agreed to sign the first treaty with a "barbarian" power in more than 200 years. A convention signed on March 31, 1854, opened the ports of Shimoda and Hakodate to American ships for the supply of coal and stores.

For 10 years Japan's rulers vacillated over how to deal with the foreign threat. They did not immediately adopt a wholehearted policy of concession, but by the 1860's a whole series of "unequal treaties" was in place. The United States, Britain, France, and the Netherlands all won commercial privileges, residence rights for foreigners, the presence of diplomatic representatives, and restrictions on the Japanese export of opium. In 1868 the shogunate collapsed, having lost its credibility by being unable to withstand the might of the "barbarians."

Perry's letter, and that of the president, had started a momentous change. The old imperial court resumed power, dedicated to wiping out Japan's inferiority to the West. There developed a mania for Western ideas. Advanced technologies were mastered and incorporated. Antiforeign agitation was dropped in favor of learning from the West the secrets of its strength. By the end of the 19th century the Japanese progressed so rapidly that they had an army and navy powerful enough to win a war with Russia in 1904–05.

Henry Morton Stanley
TO
The New York Herald

April 14, 1875

*The renowned explorer of Africa
enthusiastically proposes that missionaries be sent
to convert the people of Buganda.*

*Stanley in 1885, after
claiming the Congo (now
Zaire) for the king of Belgium.*

In 1874 the 33-year-old Henry Morton Stanley set out on an expedition across Africa that lasted 999 days. Stanley's aim was to clinch his claim to be the greatest explorer of the "Dark Continent." Already world famous from his "discovery" of Dr. David Livingstone at Ujiji on Lake Tanganyika in 1871, Stanley headed a lavishly equipped and financed expedition, with 350 porters and riflemen. The enormous expenses of the enterprise were borne jointly by the *New York Herald*, which employed Stanley, and London's *Daily Telegraph*. The arrangement was that Stanley's reports would appear first in the *Herald* and then a few days later in the *Telegraph*. This letter, published seven months after it was written, was carried by porters to Zanzibar off the east coast of Africa, and from there by sea to New York.

During this expedition Stanley became the first to circumnavigate Lakes Victoria and Tanganyika, the first to chart the River Lualaba, and the first to follow the course of the River Congo to its Atlantic estuary. From November 1874 to March 1875 he made a grueling march from the East African coast at Zanzibar to Buganda in the northwestern area of Lake Victoria (equivalent to about half of modern Uganda). Half his force died, prey to disease and hostile tribesmen. But once in Buganda, Stanley began to grow in confidence. Mutesa, the kabaka (king), had already encountered explorer John Speke in 1862, and he received Stanley hospitably.

Above: A gold medal presented to Stanley by the British Royal Geographical Society in 1890.

Left: The issue of the New York Herald *in which the letter appeared.*

I had almost neglected to inform you and your readers of one very interesting subject connected with Mutesa which will gratify many a philanthropic European and American. Until I arrived at Mutesa's court the king delighted in the idea that he was a follower of Islam; but by one conversation I flatter myself that I have tumbled the newly raised religious fabric to the ground, and, if it were only followed by the arrival of a Christian mission here, the conversion of Mutesa and his court to Christianity would be complete. But, O that some pious, practical missionary would come here! What a field and a harvest ripe for the sickle of the Gospel! Mutesa would give him anything he desired—houses, lands, cattle, ivory, &c. He might call a province his own in one day. It is not the mere preacher that is wanted here. The bishops of all Great Britain collected, with all the classic youth of Oxford and Cambridge, would effect nothing here with the intelligent people of Buganda. It is the practical Christian, who can cure their diseases, construct dwellings, understands agriculture and can turn his hand to anything, like a sailor—this is the man that is wanted here. Such a man, if he can be found, would become the savior of Africa. Now where is there in all the pagan world a more promising field for a mission?

With permission I would suggest that the mission should bring to Mutesa as presents three or four suits of military clothes, decorated freely with gold embroidery, with half a dozen French képis, a saber, a brace of pistols and suitable ammunition, a good fowling piece and rifle of good quality, as the king is not a barbarian; a cheap dinner service of Britannia ware, an iron bedstead and counterpanes, a few pieces of cotton print, boots, &c. For trade it should bring the blue, black and gray woolen cloths, a quantity of military buttons, gold braid and cord, silk cord of different colors, as well as binding, linen and sheeting for shirts, fine red blankets and a quantity of red cloth, a few chairs and tables. The profit arising from the sale of these things would be enormous.

Henry M. Stanley

These extracts from Stanley's first letter to *The Herald* from Mutesa's court boldly announce that the kabaka wanted to convert from Islam to Christianity. Hospitality aside, Mutesa had no intention of converting, but he did recognize the advantages of closer contact with Europeans, not least in the technology of war. Mutesa's true concern focused on the threat to his kingdom from Egypt. The British soldier General Charles George Gordon, employed as governor of Equatoria (southern Sudan) by the khedive Ismail Pasha of Egypt, was anxious to extend Egyptian power into the Bantu areas to the south. Mutesa explained to Stanley his principal motive for "conversion": the white man's military technology was superior to that of the Arab slavers who had introduced Islam into Central Africa, so the white man's "magic book" must be superior to the Koran.

Despite his great achievements, Stanley had his faults, and the letter to the *Herald* points up two of his shortcomings. He was a publicity seeker, a devotee of "good copy," and he saw that he would achieve a great publicity coup if he could declare that a vast area of Central Africa was cry-

Above: Bishop Achte of the White Fathers in 1890, with novice brothers. Their Maltese crosses commemorate training in Malta.

ing out for missionary work. He also tended to overrate his personal charisma and persuasiveness, and to imagine that he possessed an unusual ability to win people to his point of view; it did not occur to him, as long as they appeared deferential, that they might be duping him. Until his death in 1884 Mutesa stalled and kept the missionaries who flocked into Buganda dangling, though many people converted. Mutesa's son Mwanga soon saw the Christian converts as a threat and acquired the reputation of an African Nero by his persecutions, culminating in the murder of Bishop James Hannington in 1885. Mwanga gave Christian converts the choice of recanting; if they refused, they were castrated and roasted alive. When this proved too slow-working, Mwanga ordered Christian converts to be burned at the stake in batches.

When Mwanga's excesses triggered his deposition in 1888 and civil war in Buganda, Stanley was returning from an armed expedition to the Sudan. His force had the most up-to-date weaponry but was exhausted, and Stanley did not turn aside to help the Bugandan Christians.

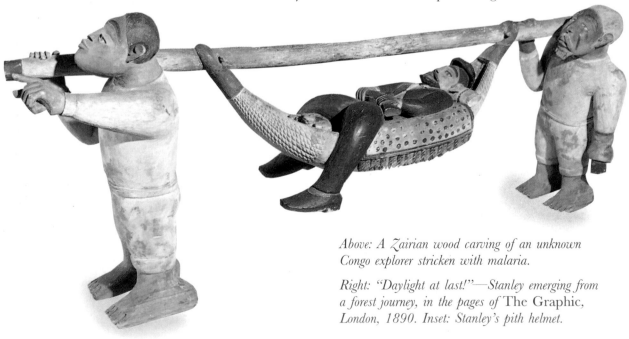

Above: A Zairian wood carving of an unknown Congo explorer stricken with malaria.

Right: "Daylight at last!"—Stanley emerging from a forest journey, in the pages of The Graphic, *London, 1890. Inset: Stanley's pith helmet.*

LOUIS PASTEUR
TO
HIS FAMILY

June 2, 1881

*The French chemist and biologist reports
exciting progress in the first full-scale scientific attempt
to use a vaccine against disease.*

Surrounded by his family in their garden at Anbois, summer 1892.

 y the mid-1860's Louis Pasteur, effective founder of the modern studies of bacteriology, microbiology, and immunology, had made valuable discoveries in yeast fermentation, lactic acid-producing microbes, and tartrate crystals. To help the French wine industry to combat spoilage, he had also developed the process of pasteurization.

Pasteur achieved the breakthrough leading to the events described in this letter when, in 1879, he inoculated healthy chickens with an old chicken cholera culture, which had lain forgotten in a cupboard for several weeks. He made a sensational discovery: the chickens sickened but did not die and, when inoculated with a fresh culture, proved to have become resistant to the disease. The principle of vaccination had been scientifically confirmed: inoculation with a weak culture of a specific disease-causing microbe provided resistance against a strong culture of the same strain.

Pasteur set out to discover whether sheep and cows vaccinated with the weakened bacilli of anthrax were also protected from the normal fatal results of subsequent inoculation with a virulent strain. In 1881 he tried out his vaccine of anthrax bacteria on 50 sheep. As he triumphantly wrote to his children, the vaccinated animals survived. In addition to proving the effectiveness of vaccination, Pasteur now offered incontrovertible

Above: This caricature of Pasteur appeared in 1882, the year following his breakthrough.

Left: A commander of the Legion of Honor, Pasteur wore the "grand" cross of the Legion.

Biography

*L*ouis Pasteur (1822–95), born in Dôle, studied at Besançon and Paris. He held academic posts at Strasbourg, Lille, and Paris, and in 1867 became professor of chemistry at the Sorbonne, Paris. His great strengths as a researcher were his patience, his curiosity, and the ability to make connections where no one had seen them before. Famous as much for his pioneering work with vaccines as for the process of pasteurization that bears his name, he founded the Pasteur Institute in 1888 to carry on his fight against disease.

It is only Thursday, and I am already writing to you; it is because a great result is now acquired. A wire from Melun has just announced it. On Tuesday last, 31st May, we inoculated all the sheep, vaccinated and non-vaccinated, with very virulent splenic fever. It is not forty-eight hours ago. Well, the telegram tells me that, when we arrive at two o'clock this afternoon, all the non-vaccinated subjects will be dead; eighteen were already dead this morning, and the others dying. As to the vaccinated ones, they are all well; the telegram ends by the words "stunning success" it is from the veterinary surgeon, M. Rossignol.

It is too early yet for a final judgment. But if all goes well, they will henceforth preserve their good health, and the success will indeed have been startling. On Tuesday, we had a foretaste of the final results. On Saturday and Sunday, two sheep had been abstracted from the lot of twenty-five vaccinated sheep, and two from the lot of twenty-five non-vaccinated ones, and inoculated with a very virulent virus. Now, when on Tuesday all the visitors arrived, we found the two unvaccinated sheep dead, and the two others in good health. I then said to one of the veterinary surgeons who were present, "Did I not read in a newspaper, signed by you, à propos the virulent little organism of saliva, 'There! one more microbe; when there are 100 we shall make a cross.'" "It is true," he immediately answered, honestly. "But I am a converted and repentant sinner." Joy reigns in the laboratory and in the house.

Rejoice dear children.

L. Pasteur

evidence of the germ theory of disease—that a specific micro-organism causes a specific disease.

Pasteur went on to develop vaccines against swine fever and rabies. By the culture of antitoxic reagents, effective treatment of diphtheria, tuberculosis, cholera, yellow fever, and plague was eventually developed.

It must have been with particular poignancy that Pasteur announced his triumph to his two surviving children: of his five children, three had died in childhood, one at the age of nine. When Pasteur tried out his antirabies vaccine, it was on

Above: Pasteur's spectacles.

Below: Pasteur used a similar syringe to vaccinate the sheep.

Joseph Meister, a nine-year-old boy who survived the vaccinations and lived on to work at the Pasteur Institute. He eventually became gatekeeper of this enduring monument to the man whose intellect, perseverance, and dedication made him a savior to millions.

ALBERT EINSTEIN
TO
FRANKLIN D. ROOSEVELT

August 2, 1939

The great scientist puts the authoritative signature to a colleague's plea to the U.S. president to begin research into nuclear weapons.

Albert Einstein, the pacifist who advocated construction of the atomic bomb.

Franklin Delano Roosevelt, the president who took Einstein's advice.

In November, 1954, just a year before his death, Albert Einstein voiced a regret while in conversation with the Nobel Prize-winning physicist Linus Pauling: "I made one great mistake in my life—when I signed the letter to President Roosevelt recommending that atom bombs be made. But there was some justification—the danger that the Germans would make them."

In 1939, four weeks before Hitler invaded Poland, Einstein sent F.D.R. the letter abbreviated here. Already the 20th-century's most famous scientist, Einstein was at this stage still skeptical that the discovery of uranium fission meant that high-energy atomic bombs could be made. The idea behind producing nuclear energy by splitting the uranium atom was to bombard the nucleus of the atom with neutrons. It had been discovered that when the nucleus of a uranium atom was penetrated by a neutron, it behaved like an overloaded drop of water and split in two. The two new atoms combined were lighter than the original one by one-fifth, for part of the mass had been converted into energy. A further breakthrough came when a reaction was discovered in which the impact of a neutron produced secondary neutrons, which in turn produced others in an energy-producing chain reaction.

The physicist Niels Bohr was anxious about the potential of a bomb manufactured by nuclear chain reaction. But his colleague Leo Szilard, a Hungarian-born scientist working in the United States, had more immediate concerns. Szilard, particularly worried that Germany might get hold of the stocks of

Above: Einstein became a U.S. citizen at this ceremony in 1940.

Biography

Albert Einstein (1879–1955), German-born physicist, revolutionized the human conception of the nature of the universe. His first, special theory of relativity (1905) stated that matter could be converted into energy in previously unsuspected ways, that motion and rest were part of the same reality, and that space and time could not be understood apart from each other but only as a four-dimensional space-time continuum. In his general theory of relativity he refined the Newtonian idea of gravity—for example, accepting light to be affected by gravity. A lifelong pacifist and Zionist, Einstein left Germany when the Nazis came to power and spent the rest of his life in the United States.

municated to me in manuscript, leads me to expect
ium may be turned into a new and important source

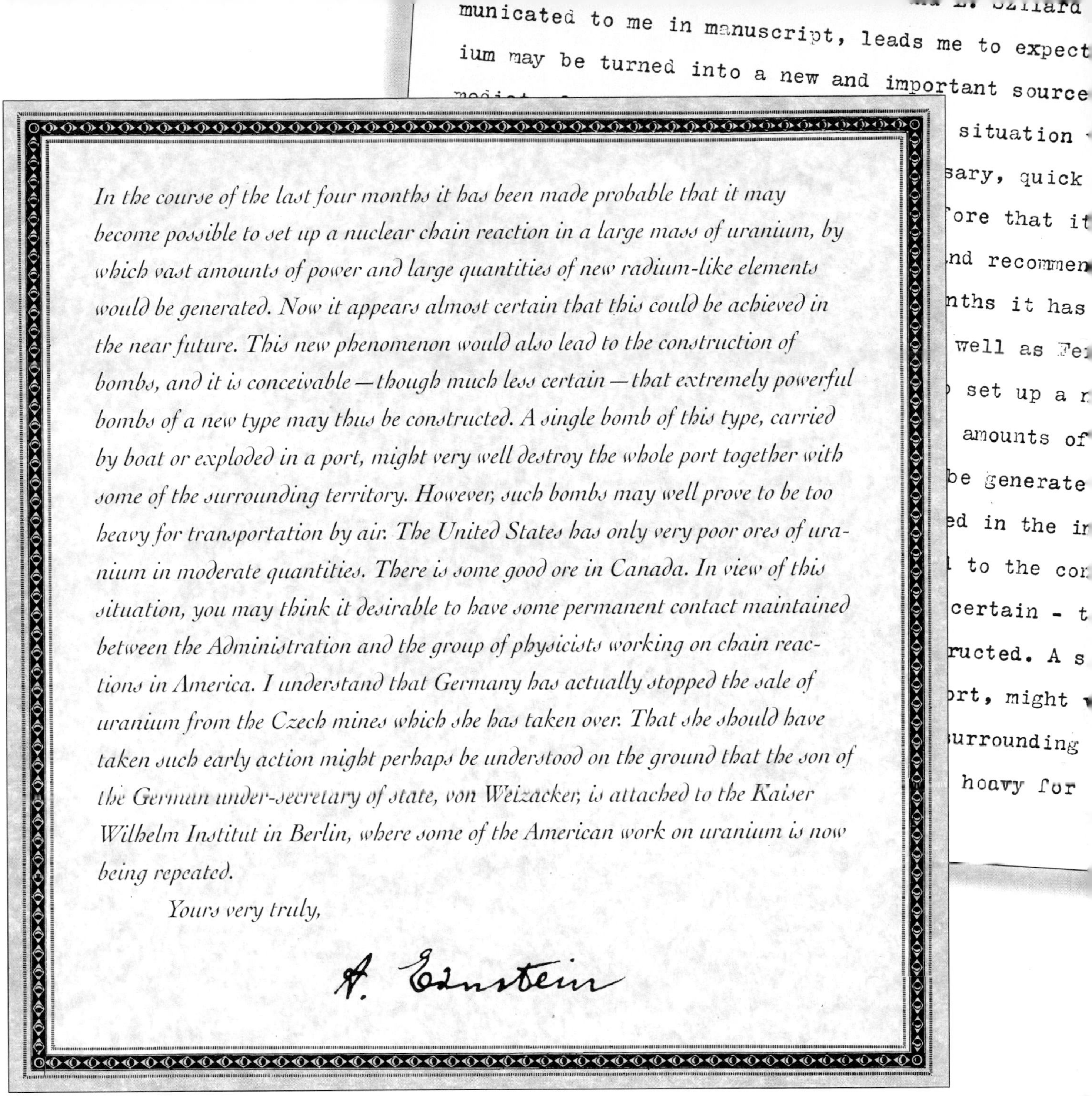

In the course of the last four months it has been made probable that it may become possible to set up a nuclear chain reaction in a large mass of uranium, by which vast amounts of power and large quantities of new radium-like elements would be generated. Now it appears almost certain that this could be achieved in the near future. This new phenomenon would also lead to the construction of bombs, and it is conceivable—though much less certain—that extremely powerful bombs of a new type may thus be constructed. A single bomb of this type, carried by boat or exploded in a port, might very well destroy the whole port together with some of the surrounding territory. However, such bombs may well prove to be too heavy for transportation by air. The United States has only very poor ores of uranium in moderate quantities. There is some good ore in Canada. In view of this situation, you may think it desirable to have some permanent contact maintained between the Administration and the group of physicists working on chain reactions in America. I understand that Germany has actually stopped the sale of uranium from the Czech mines which she has taken over. That she should have taken such early action might perhaps be understood on the ground that the son of the German under-secretary of state, von Weizacker, is attached to the Kaiser Wilhelm Institut in Berlin, where some of the American work on uranium is now being repeated.

Yours very truly,

A. Einstein

uranium held by the Belgian company *Union Minière* in the Belgian Congo, decided to warn the American president of the danger.

Although the letter is signed by Einstein, it was almost entirely Szilard's work. In fact, the Hungarian wrote two letters, both dated August 2, and sent them to Einstein. Einstein in turn signed and returned them, telling Szilard to use whichever he thought the more effective.

Szilard opted for the version that appears here. The influential economist Alexander Sachs, who was an acquaintance of Szilard's and had the ear of the president, acted as intermediary. Sachs delivered the letter to the president on October 11, together with a memorandum of his own, outlining the dangers as he saw them.

Roosevelt responded characteristically to this overture. He said to Sachs, "Alex, what you are after is to see that the Nazis don't blow us up." Sachs replied: "Precisely." As a result of the meeting Roosevelt set up the Briggs Committee to decide on a future U.S. nuclear program.

The investigation of the military use of nuclear energy made slow progress, so in

February 1940, Einstein wrote again, this time to Sachs, asking him to alert President Roosevelt that Germany's interest in uranium appeared to have intensified.

When the White House did not seem to be acting with the necessary dispatch, Einstein wrote yet again to Sachs (April 25, 1940); this time his lobbying led to the reorganization of the Briggs Committee and a serious commitment to the atomic weapons program. The crucial decision to follow laboratory work with industrial exploitation was taken in 1942 with the start-up of the highly secret multimillion-dollar Manhattan Project, committed to building a bomb.

The Germans meanwhile, still at this stage sweeping all before them in the war, decided not to investigate this avenue of research. The reasons are obscure, but one recent theory is that the

Above: Physicists observe the first sustained chain reaction, on December 2, 1942, at the University of Chicago.

Right: This first-ever color photograph of an atomic explosion was made at a test in New Mexico in 1946.

Far Right: The watch of a Hiroshima victim, which stopped forever at 8:15 A.M. on August 6, 1945.

Below: The equipment the German physicist Otto Hahn used to split the atom in 1938.

patriotic but anti-Nazi Werner Heisenberg, who headed German atomic research, advised them that it was not practicable, with available resources, to build an atomic bomb.

Therein lies the irony. Einstein, a lifelong pacifist, had been spurred into advocating the building of an atomic bomb solely through fear that the Nazis might construct one first.

Einstein himself played no part in the development of the Manhattan Project, though he was no doubt aware of its progress in general terms. The breakthrough was the discovery that bombarding uranium in a chain-reacting pile would produce a new, easily separated element, plutonium, which could be used in a bomb.

On July 16, 1945, the first atomic bomb was successfully tested in New Mexico, and on August 6 the first bomb was used in warfare on the Japanese city of Hiroshima, killing at least 70,000 people and devastating the city. The era of potential global destruction had arrived.

Einstein himself opposed using the bomb against Japan, arguing that the Japanese should first be invited to witness its destructive powers on an uninhabited island.

Einstein has been accused by posterity of a muddled and ambivalent attitude toward the atom bomb, but his position was always quite clear. He consistently argued that the Nazis were an exception to his general rule of pacifism, and that their force must be met with force.

It followed that if there was a danger that the Nazis might develop a weapon based on uranium fission, the Allies should develop it first. But Einstein felt that the loss of about 130,000 lives at Hiroshima and Nagasaki went beyond his utilitarian formula of "minimal force to achieve desired moral ends." After the war he campaigned for proper control of the atom bomb and its successor, the hydrogen bomb.

Fear of a global holocaust caused by a weapon that humans had created but could not control remained an abiding concern to the end of Einstein's life. "Science has brought forth this danger," he said, "but the real problem is in the hearts and minds of men."

SELF-PORTRAITS
&
JUSTIFICATIONS

Most people are convinced that they are driven by good motives; few see themselves as genuinely evil. However, men and women have often had to defend themselves against enemies seeking to blacken their names. The ringing self-justification thrown in the face of one's accusers is a familiar feature of the historical record. Sometimes this appears in the form of autobiography, sometimes in fine rhetoric delivered on a public rostrum or in a court of law. On occasion, especially when the victim has been deprived of an opportunity to speak out publicly, such self-justification takes the form of a letter written to a friend or to the man or woman sitting on the seat of judgment.

It is usually those people endowed with considerable self-confidence who can write memorably in this way, and the power of their argument often transcends any unfavorable circumstances they may have brought upon themselves. Thus Marie Antoinette, whose thoughtlessness had contributed to the French people's fury with the Bourbon dynasty, and whose enemies had accused her of the grotesque crime of incest with her own son in order to ensure her death sentence, wrote a moving letter of self-defense a few hours before her execution. Yet even in this final, touching moment she showed little understanding of what had brought her to such a pass.

In the case of Dante proudly refusing a degrading release from exile, we are given both a lucid picture of the injustice of a situation and of the writer's comprehensive appreciation of his own worth. Even more remarkable—because of being far more more clearheaded in his appreciation of the forces ranged against him—was the uneducated American immigrant Bartolomeo Vanzetti, also writing shortly before he was due to be executed along with his compatriot as the result of what many felt was a trumped-up charge and prejudice.

Not all letters of self-justification are written in such extreme circumstances, though many inevitably reflect turning points in a career, or perhaps in history itself. Martin Luther may have been unaware of it at the time, but his letter to the pope justifying his criticisms of the church and protesting that he never meant to challenge papal authority itself, would serve as the beginning of the greatest attack on the papacy and the established church in history. Washington, in replying with revulsion to the suggestion that he reestablish a monarchy, moved America irrevocably along its path toward true independence.

Some letters come from the young, eager for the chance to begin their careers or to be given the break that they desire. In 1745 Bonnie Prince Charlie wrote impatiently to his father James, who was advocating caution in the plan to restore the Stuarts to the thrones of England and Scotland; 140 years later the youthful and ambitious William Randolph Hearst vigorously outlined his plans to become a newspaper magnate to his father, demanding to be set up in his chosen career.

Hearst's equally energetic contemporary Thomas Edison approached his parents more sympathetically, while another imaginative genius from an earlier age, the young Leonardo da Vinci, wrote in a deferential vein to the duke of Milan, claiming for himself remarkable skills as a great military engineer who might also be employed as a painter. Leonardo's letter is a classic example of a genre even more familiar to us today: the letter begging for work, containing a résumé carefully angled toward the presumed needs of the potential employer.

DANTE
TO
A FRIEND

1315

After 14 years in exile, Dante proudly spurns the degrading terms of his pardon and recall to Florence.

Dante's death mask, made when he died in Ravenna, still in exile.

 he greatest of all Italian poets, Dante Alighieri, is best remembered for *The Divine Comedy* and *The Vita Nuova*. In *The Vita Nuova* he immortalizes his idealized love for a girl glimpsed first when both were nine years old, Beatrice Portinari. She married another man and died in 1290 at 24. As in his personal life, so in his political life: Dante was destined to see his ideals disappointed.

Italy in the late 13th century was riven by factional fighting between Guelfs and Ghibellines. The Guelfs, the party of the middle classes, supported the pope and wanted to keep the Holy Roman Emperor (the ruler of Germany) out of Italy. The Ghibellines, mainly the military and court aristocracy, backed the emperor. In Dante's native Florence there was a further complication: this Guelf city was divided between Black or "pure" Guelfs and White or disaffected Guelfs, who eventually made common cause with the Ghibellines. Dante, who sat in one of the councils of civic government, took part in suppressing both brands of factionalism.

When Charles de Valois, brother of the king of France, intervened in Florence in 1301 and put the Blacks in power, Dante was among the old enemies banished by the city's new rulers. In January 1302 Dante and three other exiles were charged with corrupt practice in office and conspiracy against Charles de Valois, the pope, and the peace of Florence. On March 10, 1302, they were condemned *in absentia* to be burned alive, but in 1315 word was sent that the exiles could safely return to Florence

Above: Dante and Virgil on their way to Purgatory in The Divine Comedy.

Biography

Dante Alighieri (1265–1321), Florentine poet, philosopher, and politician, was born and raised a lawyer's son in Florence. Dante married Gemma Donati, of a noble Guelf family, and had seven children. On the losing side in the complex political struggle between Guelf factions, Dante was exiled in 1302 and settled in 1318 in Ravenna. He may be said to be the founder of Italian—particularly Tuscan dialect—as a literary language. *The Divine Comedy*, Dante's greatest work, occupied him for most of the last 20 years of his life. This allegory of the Christian way to God describes the journey through Hell and Purgatory to Paradise, both for the individual soul and for the community.

From your letter, which I received with due respect and affection, and have diligently studied, I learn with gratitude how my recall to Florence has been the object of your care and concern; and I am the more beholden to you therefore, inasmuch as it rarely happens that an exile finds friends.

I gather, then, from the letter of your nephew and mine I may receive pardon, and be permitted to return forthwith, on condition that I pay a certain sum of money, and submit to the stigma of the oblation — two propositions, my father, which in sooth are as ridiculous as they are ill advised — ill advised, that is to say, on the part of those who have communicated them, for in your letter, which was more discreetly and cautiously formulated, no hint of such conditions was conveyed.

This, then, is the gracious recall of Dante Alighieri to his native city, after the miseries of well-nigh fifteen years of exile!

This is the reward of innocence manifest to all the world, and of the sweat and toil of unremitting study! No! my father, not by this path will I return to my native city.

If some other can be found, in the first place by yourself and thereafter by others, which does not derogate from the fame and honor of Dante, that will I tread with no lagging steps. But if by no such path Florence may be entered, then will I enter Florence never.

What! Can I not anywhere gaze upon the face of the sun and stars? Can I not under any sky contemplate the most precious truths, without first returning to Florence, disgraced, nay dishonored, in the eyes of my fellow citizens? Assuredly bread will not fail me!

DANTE

Right: Restored to the city's esteem, Dante appears center-stage, reading from his works, in this 15th-century fresco in Florence Cathedral.

on payment of a fine and submission to the ceremony of "oblation": carrying a candle and wearing sackcloth and a miter, they would be taken from prison to the Baptistery, where approved sponsors would "offer" them at the altar to Saint John the Baptist and to God. In these excerpts from a letter to a Florentine priest, probably his brother-in-law Teruccio di Manetto Donati, Dante, who was never to return from exile, scornfully rejects the terms of his pardon.

LEONARDO DA VINCI
TO
THE DUKE OF MILAN

1482

*Perhaps the finest artist in the
history of the world seeks employment
as a military engineer.*

*Leonardo da
Vinci, who
considered that
Milan had a
pressing need for
his skills as a
military engineer.*

*The Duke of
Milan, (called
"il Moro," the
Moor, because of
his dark
complexion), who
wanted an artist.*

arly in 1482 Leonardo left Florence, where he had worked and studied since his youth. He went to Milan on the advice of Lorenzo de' Medici. This patron of the greatest artists of the day had been asked by Lodovico, Duke of Milan, to recommend someone to cast a bronze equestrian statue of his father Francesco, founder of the Sforza dynasty. Leonardo was attracted by Lodovico's reputation as a wealthy and generous patron, lord of the richest city in Italy.

In Leonardo's judgment, military engineering was the most pressing need of the ruler of an Italian city-state in troubled times, and the letter by which he introduced himself to the duke emphasized this element of his highly versatile genius. Yet in the process he played down those talents Lodovico would have found most appealing. The duke was aware that Milan lagged behind Rome and Venice artistically and wanted to change this by attracting artists and scholars to his court. Indeed, when Lorenzo de' Medici wrote on Leonardo's behalf, concentrating on his skills as lyre player and singer, he was closer to the mark. Consequently, the artist's letter went unanswered at first. It was apparently an altar painting of "Madonna of the Rocks" that actually drew Lodovico's attention. He then employed Leonardo officially as painter and engineer.

Some of the proposals set out in Leonardo's letter held the promise of a dramatic leap forward in military technology. Lodovico had no

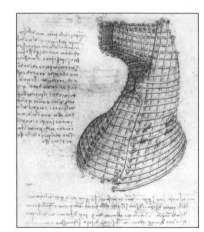

*Leonardo's sketch of the
superstructure for a clay
model of Francesco's
horse—never completed.*

Biography

*L*eonardo, born in 1452 in the Tuscan town of Vinci, was the original Renaissance man. He distinguished himself as a painter, engineer, architect and scientist. He produced some of the greatest paintings and cartoons (sketches for paintings) ever made: "Virgin and Child with St. Anne," "The Last Supper," "Battle of Anghiari," "Mona Lisa," "Madonna of the Rocks." He did memorable work as a sculptor, devised a system of irrigation for the plains of Lombardy, directed court pageants and produced some highly original work in hydrodynamics, biology, physiology, and aeronautics. Leonardo died in France in 1519, at the age of 67.

Having, most illustrious lord, seen and considered the experiments of those who pose as masters in the art of inventing instruments of war, and found that their inventions differ in no way from those in common use, I am emboldened, without any prejudice to anyone, to seek an appointment for showing your Excellency certain of my secrets.

1. I can construct bridges which are very light and strong and portable, with which to pursue and defeat the enemy; and others more solid, which resist fire or assault yet are easily removed and placed in position.

2. In the case of a siege I can cut off water from the trenches and make pontoons and scaling ladders and other similar contrivances.

3. I can also make a cannon which is light and easy to transport, with which to hurl small stones like hail, and whose smoke causes great terror to the enemy so that they suffer heavy losses and confusion.

4. I can make armored wagons to carry artillery, able to break through the strongest enemy lines and to open a safe passage for the infantry.

5. I can construct cannon and mortar and light ordnance in shape both ornamental and useful, and different from those in common use.

6. Where it is impossible to use cannon, I can supply instead catapults, mangonels, trabocchi and other instruments not in general use. In short, as the occasion demands, I can supply infinite means of attack and defense.

7. If the fight should take place upon the sea I can construct many engines most suitable either for attack or defense.

8. In times of peace, I believe that I can give you as complete satisfaction as anyone in the construction of buildings both public and private, and in transporting water from one place to another.

       I can further execute sculpture in marble, bronze and clay, also in painting I can do as much as anyone else, whoever he may be.

       Moreover, I would undertake the commission of the bronze horse, which shall endue with immortal glory and eternal honor the auspicious memory of your father and of the illustrious house of Sforza.

Leonardo da Vinci

Right: These wheeled engines of war, suggestive of the tank and the armored car, got no farther than Leonardo's highly prolific drawing board.

Left: The French invasion meant that the bronze for Leonardo's equestrian statue of Francesco had to be diverted to cannon making.

Below: A reconstruction of Leonardo's idea for a man-powered flying machine.

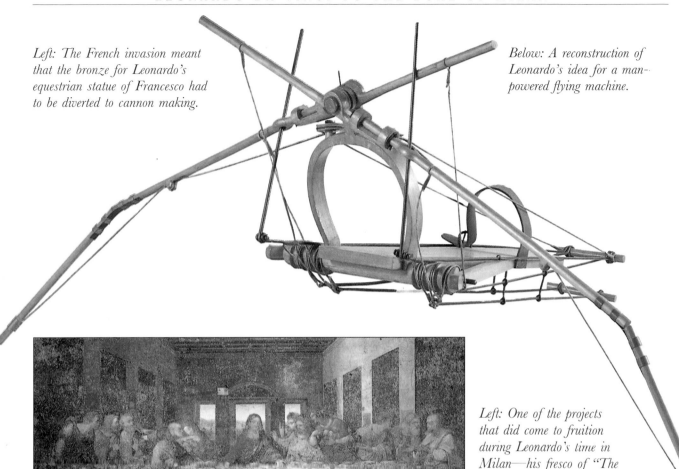

Left: One of the projects that did come to fruition during Leonardo's time in Milan—his fresco of "The Last Supper."

interest in such advances, choosing instead to use diplomacy to checkmate his enemies. In so doing he violated the rules soon to be laid down by Niccolò Machiavelli in *The Prince*, the notorious handbook on gaining and retaining power. One clear message stood out among Machiavelli's rules: if you wish for peace, prepare for war.

Lodovico had reduced the rightful ruler of Milan, his nephew Gian Galleazzo, to a puppet, but when the young man died in 1494 his supporters threatened to rise against the usurper. Lodovico called in the French as allies but five years later they too turned on him and carried him off to France as a prisoner in an iron cage. French soldiers used the clay model Leonardo had built of the horse in the planned equestrian bronze of Francesco for target practice.

Leonardo apparently resolved to choose patrons whose grasp on power was more secure: the next man to commission him was the ruler admired by Machiavelli—Cesare Borgia, conqueror of the Romagna region of northern Italy.

Among the schemes flowing from the fertile brain of Leonardo da Vinci, only to be ignored by his various patrons, were a brothel cunningly decorated on the outside to provide secret entries for clients; a plan for revolutionizing the sewerage and drainage system of Milan to prevent malaria; two-level streets, with the upper tier reserved for the nobility; windmills with revolving roofs; printing presses, diving bells, diving suits, automatic doors, alarm clocks, and flying machines.

The career of Leonardo reminds us of two familiar lessons: the need for patrons if great art is to be, and the accelerated rate of cultural achievement in times of violent change. Patronage may flourish in settled conditions; but, as Orson Welles pointed out, "In Italy for 30 years under the Borgias they had warfare, terror, murder, bloodshed—they produced Michelangelo, Leonardo da Vinci and the Renaissance. In Switzerland they had brotherly love, five hundred years of democracy and peace, and what did that produce? The cuckoo clock."

MARTIN LUTHER
TO
POPE LEO X

September 6, 1518

*The archcritic of the Catholic Church
argues that he never sought to challenge
the authority of the pope.*

*Martin Luther,
who did not intend
to break with the
Catholic Church.*

*Leo X (Giovanni
de' Medici), who
underestimated the
threat that Luther
posed.*

 n 1517 a German monk and theologian, Martin Luther, became disturbed by the abuse of indulgences—the remission of punishment still due for sin after sacramental absolution. He composed a list of objections to this and other church practices, and sent it to his bishop and to his archbishop. He nailed the list—his famous 95 Theses (topics for debate)—to the door of the church at Wittenberg.

Luther had no revolutionary aspirations; he certainly could have had no idea that his action would spark off the decisive split in the church known as the Reformation.

Biography

Martin Luther (1483–1546), whose seal appears at left, was educated at the university and Augustinian monastery at Erfurt, and soon displayed formidable gifts as a theologian. Luther's condemnation of the sale of indulgences in 1517 set him on a collision course with the church that resulted ultimately in his excommunication. He continued to work and to preach reform but no longer tried to reconcile his theological views with those of the Catholic hierarchy in Rome. Luther's later writings diverged greatly from Catholic teaching. The principle of salvation through grace and justification by faith, as he espoused it, became a key element in the theological framework of Protestantism.

The sale of indulgences was a widespread practice throughout the Catholic Church. By opposing it, Luther had already made himself unpopular with his own ruler, the elector of Saxony, who made money from it. The scale of the jubilee indulgence, launched to raise money toward rebuilding St. Peter's in Rome, and the unseemly enthusiasm of the Dominican monk Johann Tetzel, who had the commission to raise money in Germany by peddling indulgences, provoked Luther to take direct action. Luther's Theses denounced papal venality, claimed the pope has no jurisdiction over purgatory, and denied altogether the validity of indulgences.

*Above: The Devil's bagpipe,
a 1525 caricature of Luther.*

*Right: The 1520 papal bull
condemning Luther's views.*

Luther regarded himself not as a heretic but as a reformer of such abuses from within the church. However, when Pope Leo X summoned

It has come to my attention that I am accused of great indiscretion, said to be my great fault, in which, it is said, I have not spared even your person.

I beg you to give me a hearing after I have vindicated myself by this letter, and believe me when I say that I have never thought ill of you personally.

I have truly despised your see, the Roman Curia, which, however, neither you nor anyone else can deny is more corrupt than any Babylon or Sodom ever was, and which, as far as I can see, is characterized by a completely depraved, hopeless, and notorious godlessness.

I have been thoroughly incensed over the fact that good Christians are mocked in your name and under the cloak of the Roman church.

I have always been sorry, most excellent Leo, that you were made pope in these times, for you are worthy of being pope in better days.

So far have I been from raving against your person that I even hoped I might gain your favor and save you if I should make a strong and stinging assault upon that prison, that veritable hell of yours.

So I come, most blessed father, and, prostrate before you, pray that if possible you intervene and stop those flatterers, who are the enemies of peace while they pretend to keep peace. But let no person imagine that I will recant unless he prefer to involve the whole question in even greater turmoil.

Furthermore, I acknowledge no fixed rules for the interpretation of the Word of God, since the Word of God, which teaches freedom in all other matters, must not be bound.

Perhaps I am presumptuous in trying to instruct so exalted a personage from whom we all should learn and from whom the thrones of judges receive their decisions, as those pestilential fellows of yours boast. But I do not consider it absurd if I now forget your exalted office and do what brotherly love demands.

May the Lord Jesus preserve you forever. Amen.

Martinus Luther

Bulla contra errores Martini Lutheri z sequacium.

Above: Luther's reformed Christianity (left) and Roman corruption (right) as seen by the Protestant artist Lucas Cranach the Elder (1472–1553).

him to Rome to explain his behavior, Luther declined to go, fearing death or imprisonment. He appealed to the elector of Saxony, Frederick the Wise, to intervene. Jealous of his own authority, Frederick was determined to protect Luther against Rome as a matter of principle as well as politics. It was settled with Cardinal Cajetan, the papal legate to Saxony, that a personal interview would be held at Augsburg.

Cajetan held a weak hand. Forced to offer Luther safe-conduct to the interview, his only course of action once there was that of gentle persuasion to get Luther to retract. When Luther refused, the cardinal lost his temper and the interview ended in chaos.

After Augsburg, Luther's break with Rome

was inevitable, yet Leo at first underestimated the threat to his authority from the disturbances in Germany. He believed that Luther's defiance might be read simply as traditional German unease with papal authority; after all, when Cajetan had asked the Diet (parliament) of Augsburg in 1518 for a special tax to finance a new crusade, the Diet had replied that the real enemy of Christendom was not the Turk but the "hellhound" in Rome.

In addition, political considerations required Leo to adopt a cautious attitude toward events in

Above: The Wartburg, the castle where Frederick the Wise kept Luther safe for 10 months in 1521–22.

Below: A first edition of the German translation of the Bible Luther made during his refuge at the Wartburg.

Saxony. On the death of Maximilian, the Holy Roman Emperor, in 1518, there loomed the probability that the next emperor would be the Spanish Hapsburg Charles, Maximilian's grandson and later Emperor Charles V. The pope wanted to prevent the formation of a Spanish power bloc in Italy, which would combine the power of the Spanish possessions in southern Italy with the might of the German empire. This would pose a threat both to the Papal States and to Leo's native Florence. Frederick of Saxony was one of the seven electors who would choose the next emperor, and Leo was prepared to offer almost any terms to bring him over to his own side in opposing Charles.

Consequently Leo displayed a notably ambiguous attitude toward Luther. In a letter to George Spalatin, the elector's chaplain and Luther's best friend at the court of Saxony, Leo spoke of "the overbearing boldness of that only son of Satan, Friar Martin Luther . . . [who] savors of notorious heresy . . ." He deplored ". . . the rashness of the said Luther, for his erroneous doctrines, now alas! [are] sown among the credulous people." Yet in the spring of 1519 he offered to pay the expenses of a journey to Rome by "his beloved son" Luther in the hope that the rebellious priest would recant.

The pope's diplomacy failed to prevent the election of Charles as emperor in 1519. In that year, following a famous

debate in Leipzig with John Eck, Luther openly challenged the church. Opinion now swung strongly in favor of Luther, whose defiant pamphlets added fuel to the widespread German resentment toward Rome.

The third of his treatises Luther dedicated to the pope and enclosed with this letter, in which he emphasized that it was the corrupt state of the church, not the pope himself, that he felt he must challenge. Nevertheless, he was summoned under safe-conduct to be examined by Emperor Charles's ecclesiastical court (the Diet of Worms) in 1521. After his refusal to recant before this body, Luther was declared outlaw in all the imperial domains. In the same year, just before Leo X died, he added to Luther's condemnation the formal pronouncement of excommunication.

ANNE BOLEYN
TO
HENRY VIII

May 1536

Henry VIII's imprisoned second wife protests her innocence and her loyal devotion to the king.

Anne Boleyn, whose last request to the king was to spare "the Innocent Souls of those poor [accused] Gentlemen."

Henry VIII, who married Jane Seymour, his third wife, the day after Anne was beheaded.

nne Boleyn became one of the mistresses of Henry VIII of England—at a price. Henry was a man of strong personality, intellect, and will. He loved dancing, archery, and hunting, was interested in religion, and even more in eating, gambling, and women. A well-educated and alluring woman, Anne had seen her sister Mary used and discarded by the king. Anne was determined to extract a high price for her sexual favors, telling Henry, who by 1527 was besotted with her, that she would yield to him only if he married her.

Henry's first marriage had been to Catherine of Aragon, the still-virginal wife of his deceased older brother. She failed to provide Henry with the male heir that would assure the continuance of the shaky Tudor dynasty. When English policy found France more important than Spain (Catherine's country), Henry sought an annulment on the grounds of incest. He got his annulment, but only after a break with the Church of Rome, precipitating the English Reformation.

Henry finally won Anne, who was now certain of marriage, in August 1532. By the beginning of 1533 Anne was pregnant; a secret wedding took place on January 25, despite the fact that Henry had still

Biography

Anne Boleyn (c. 1504–36), second of Henry VIII's six wives, was the daughter of Sir Thomas Boleyn and Elizabeth Howard, daughter of the Duke of Norfolk. After spending a number of childhood years at the French court, she returned to England in 1522. From 1527 until 1532 Henry VIII pursued her, at first without success. Finally he agreed to make her queen, and then followed the famous "thousand days" between marriage in 1533 and execution on trumped-up charges in 1536. Anne's fate was sealed by her inability to give Henry a male heir, particularly after Pope Clement VII excommunicated Henry in 1534.

Above right: This gold pendant is believed to be Henry's first gift to Anne and in her last days she gave it to Captain Gwynne of the Guard at the Tower of London.

Left: Anne's emblem, a white falcon with Tudor roses.

Opposite: Anne Boleyn's lute.

Sir, If, as you say, confessing a Truth indeed may procure my safety, I shall with all Willingness and Duty perform your Command. But let not your Grace ever imagine that your poor Wife will ever be brought to acknowledge a Fault, where not so much as a Thought thereof proceeded. And to speak a truth, never Prince had Wife more Loyal in all Duty, and in all true Affection, than you have ever found in Anne Boleyn. Neither did I at any time so far forget myself in my received Queenship, but that I always looked for such an Alteration as now I find; for the ground of my Preferment being on no surer Foundation than your Grace's Fancy, the least Alteration, I knew, was fit and sufficient to draw that Fancy to some other Subject.

Try me good King, but let me have a Lawful Trial, and let not my sworn Enemies sit as my Accusers and Judges; yea, let me receive an open Trial, for my Truth shall fear no open shame; then shall you see, either mine Innocency cleared, your Suspicion and Conscience satisfied, the Ignominy and Slander of the World stopped, or my Guilt openly declared. So that whatsoever God or you may determine of me, your Grace may be freed from an open Censure to follow your Affection already settled on that Party, for whose sake I am now as I am. But if you have already determined of me, and that not only my Death, but an infamous Slander must bring you the enjoying of your desired Happiness; then I desire of God, that he will pardon your great Sin therein, and likewise mine Enemies, the Instruments thereof; and that he will not call you to a strict Account for your unprincely and cruel usage of me, at his General Judgment-Seat, where both you and my self must shortly appear, and in whose Judgment, I doubt not (whatsoever the World may think of me) mine Innocence shall be openly known, and sufficiently cleared.

Anne Bullen

Above: An illumination from Henry's psalter shows the king reading psalms.

Left: An unsuccessful petition to the pope for an annulment of Henry's marriage to Catherine of Aragon, with signatures and seals of compliant English bishops.

not formally divorced Catherine. Anne was crowned queen in June 1533, but almost at once cracks appeared in her relationship with Henry. The king, often unfaithful to Catherine, saw no reason to change his behavior when he changed wives. Anne, however, was less compliant than Catherine and voiced her objections. Henry grew increasingly angry at her lack of docility and deference. Anne could not see that the power she had exercised over the king during seven years of unconsummated courtship was jeopardized as soon as the king had won her. Anne's prestige and influence dimmed further when, instead of the expected son, she gave birth to a daughter (the future Elizabeth I) on August 7, 1533. There followed three miscarriages. Henry, by now thoroughly tired of her, began to regard her as dispensable. Her only hope lay in producing a son.

Nemesis arrived for Anne during a royal progress she and Henry made in the summer of 1535, when they stayed at the Seymour family home. There Henry's eye was caught by the demure and submissive Jane Seymour, one of Anne's maids of honor. Jane proved her mistress's equal in the art of submitting sexually to the king only when marriage was offered. In January 1536 Anne gave birth to a stillborn male baby. Now determined to free himself from his marriage, Henry instructed his first minister Thomas Cromwell to find a way to execute her. Cromwell came up with a charge of witchcraft against Anne, as well as adultery with five men in her household. The only evidence against her was elicited from a musician under torture.

The letter which appears here in part may have been written in the first few days of May 1536, when a weeping and hysterical Anne was first in the Tower. The letter is considered by the best scholars not to be authentic. Doubt centers on the dissimilarity between the handwriting and other known examples of Anne's penmanship. There are well-attested examples, however, of individuals in exceptionally stressful circumstances whose personalities were temporarily transformed, along with their handwriting. It is equally possible that the manuscript now in the British Museum is a copy of Anne's original letter. The document's

provenance points to its authenticity: it was found among the papers of her enemy Thomas Cromwell.

In May 1536, while Archbishop Thomas Cranmer annulled the marriage, Anne was tried by 26 browbeaten nobles afraid for their own lives. The sentence was pronounced by her own uncle, the Duke of Norfolk.

On May 17 Anne's five "lovers" were beheaded. For Anne herself Henry summoned a master headsman from France—presumably out of some residual pity for her—to ensure that the sword would cut off her head with one skillful stroke. Anne's execution was delayed for a day as a result. She went to the scaffold on May 19, 1536, protesting her innocence. It is said that as she walked to the block she kept looking back as though expecting the king's horsemen to come galloping up with a reprieve.

Henry's writing desk, decorated with symbols of his marriage to Catherine of Aragon.

Bonnie Prince Charlie
TO
James Stuart

June 12, 1745

The exiled Prince explains to his father why he is going to Scotland alone to fight for the restoration.

Charles Edward Stuart, the Young Pretender, impatient to restore the Stuart throne.

James Stuart, the Old Pretender, waiting for a more propitious moment.

When Charles Edward Stuart wrote to his father in the summer of 1745, he raised the arrogant voice of youth against cautious elders. Yet the older man, James Stuart, proved in the end to have good reasons for his caution.

When James II (Charles's grandfather) was expelled from Britain—the "Glorious Revolution" of 1688—he and his followers resolved that with the help of France they would regain the three kingdoms of England, Scotland, and Ireland for the royal house of Stuart. For the following 67 years the Jacobites—so called because the Latin for James is Jacobus—posed repeated threats to established government in Britain. James II died in 1701, but his son James (born 1688) claimed the British throne, supported by Jacobite uprisings in 1708, 1715, and 1719. James

came to be known as the "Old Pretender" when his own son, Charles Edward, emerged as the "Young Pretender." (At that time one meaning of "to pretend" was to claim). By the 1740's, Charles Edward thought his middle-aged father had lost his resolve. He believed that by raising a rebellion in Scotland he could tempt the French king, Louis XV, to revive earlier plans to invade England. The extract from Charles's letter scornfully dismisses his father's objections.

Charles went to Scotland, raised the clans, defeated the British in two major battles, and won his sobriquet of "the bonnie prince." Louis XV did revive his invasion plans, but acted too

Charlie's basket-hilted sword.

Biography

Charles Edward Stuart (1720–88) was born and brought up in Rome. The grandson of James II of England, he claimed the thrones of England, Scotland, and Ireland by strict right of succession. After his defeat in the Jacobite uprising of 1745–46, he wandered in the Scottish Highlands with a price on his head and eventually escaped to France. He then roamed Europe until 1766, when his father's death brought him back to Rome. The pope refused to recognize him as "Charles III." Increasingly embittered, Charles contracted a loveless and childless marriage, which ended in 1780 when his wife ran away with her lover. Charles, himself by now a drunkard, died eight years later.

Sir, I believe your Majesty little expected a courier at this time, and much less from me; to tell you a thing that will be a great surprise to you. I have been invited by our friends to go to Scotland; this being, they are fully persuaded, the only way of restoring you to the Crown, and them to their liberties. Had I not given my word to do so, or got so many encouragements as I have had, I should have been obliged, in honor and for my own reputation, to have flung myself into the arms of my friends, and die with them. I cannot but mention a parable here which is: a horse that is to be sold, if spurred, does not skip or show some signs of life, nobody would care to have him for nothing; just so my friends would care very little to have me, if after such usage, which all the world is sensible of, I should not show that I have life in me. Your Majesty cannot disapprove a son's following the example of his father. You yourself did the like in the year '15; but the circumstances now are indeed very different, there being a certainty of succeeding, the particulars of which would be too long to explain, and even impossible to convince you of by writing, which has been the reason that I have presumed to take upon me the managing of all this, without even letting you suspect that any such thing was brewing.

Charles P.

"The Battle of Culloden," by David Morier.

slowly, and in the meantime Charles was decisively defeated at the Battle of Culloden (April 1746). The obstacles to a restoration were greater than Charles had thought. Yet he considered that his father and the "old Jacobites" had not tried hard enough to persuade the French to send him aid. He accused them of jealousy and envy of his achievements.

Relations between father and son, always uneasy, worsened. Though he lived another 22 years, James never saw his son again. And Bonnie Prince Charlie never recovered from the disappointment of his failure in the Jacobite uprising of 1745.

GEORGE WASHINGTON
TO
COLONEL NICOLA

May 22, 1782

*The hero of the American revolution
angrily rejects the suggestion that he should take
the crown of the newly independent nation.*

Washington and his officers at Yorktown, by Louis Couder.

By the summer of 1782 George Washington was the hero of all America. Against what had sometimes seemed impossible odds, he had forced the British to surrender at Yorktown the year before. Yet it was with dismay that he received a letter from a Colonel Lewis Nicola of Pennsylvania, who proposed that Washington set himself up as king of the 13 former colonies. All major countries at the time were monarchies; and Nicola stressed that a royal government of America would be more financially respectable than that of a republic.

Biography

George Washington (1732–99) was born into a family of wealthy Virginian landowners. He represented Virginia in the 1775 Continental Congress of the American colonists, then commanded their armies in the six-year campaign against British rule that followed. He was defeated at Brandywine and Germantown, prevailed at Trenton and Princeton, and held the American army together during its darkest hour—the winter of 1777–78 in Valley Forge. After the final defeat of the British he was unanimously chosen as president of the Constitutional Convention in 1787 and was elected unopposed for two terms as the first president of the United States.

Nicola had a practical interest—he was anxious to ensure that the army and its officers were paid. The victorious Americans were faced with bankruptcy; the phrase "not worth a continental" was in common parlance, referring to the paper money issued by the Continental Congress. The army's pay was several months in arrears and the soldiers were due to return home penniless and jobless.

To Washington, steeped in the tradition of the republicanism of ancient Rome, the offer of a crown was little more than an insult. Nicola, sensing that this might be so with others, urged Washington to keep the idea quiet until the right moment came. But Nicola obviously misjudged his man when he thought Washington would react favorably.

About one thing, Nicola's judgment proved sound. The crisis over army pay was to become so bad that officers were to call a mass meeting in March 1783, which Washington had to face

Inauguration buttons from the presidential election, 1789.

Sir,

*With a mixture of great surprise and astonishment I have read
with attention the sentiments you have submitted to my perusal. Be
assured, Sir, no occurrence in the course of the War has given me more
painful sensations than your information of there being such ideas
existing in the Army as you have expressed, and I must view with
abhorrence, and reprehend with severity. For the present, the communication of
them will rest in my own bosom, unless some further agitation of the matter
shall make a disclosure necessary.*

*I am much at a loss to conceive what part of my conduct could have given
encouragement to an address which to me seems big with the greatest mischiefs
that can befall my Country. If I am not deceived in the knowledge of myself, you
could not have found a person to whom your schemes are more disagreeable—at
the same time in justice to my own feeling I must add, that no man possesses a
more sincere wish to see ample justice done to the Army than I do, and as far as
my powers and influence, in a constitutional way, may extend, they shall be
employed to the utmost of my abilities to effect it, should there be any occasion.
Let me conjure you then—if you have any regard for your Country, concern for
yourself or posterity, or respect for me—to banish these thoughts from your
mind, and never communicate, as from yourself, or anyone else, a sentiment of
the like nature.*

G. Washington

down by the force of his personality alone.

Washington's blunt answer to Nicola helped
to build him up as a national monument of
republican virtue. His biographer, Mason Weems,
linked Washington with the heroes of the ancient
world, and he was elevated virtually to sainthood
by patriots in the 19th century. Such was the
extreme reverence that a balance eventually had
to be sought. In contrast, Nathaniel Hawthorne
poked fun at the commotion over a statue of a
"Roman" George, bare to the waist in a toga.
"Did anybody ever see Washington naked?" he
asked. "It is inconceivable. He had no nakedness,
but I imagine he was born with
his clothes on, and his hair
powdered, and made a stately
bow on his first appearance in
the world."

Right: Washington's personal seal.

MARIE ANTOINETTE
TO
MADAME ELIZABETH

October 16, 1793

*The condemned queen of France writes
a tender farewell to her sister-in-law only hours
before being taken to the guillotine.*

*Marie Antoinette
in an unfinished
portrait in pastels
by Alexandre
Kucharski
(1741–1819).*

*Elizabeth, sister
of Louis XVI.
Arrested with
the royal family,
she was
guillotined in
1794.*

 he coming of the French Revolution in 1789 caught the Bourbons—the French royal family—unawares, and no one understood the new ideas and troubled times less than Louis XVI's queen, Marie Antoinette.

She had earned her people's anger with her frivolity. She schemed with Austria against France and convinced the weak-willed Louis to attempt to flee from Paris in disguise. When it was discovered, the scheme fatally discredited the monarchy. In January 1793, the king was executed.

At Marie Antoinette's trial, the revolutionaries had solid evidence in the form of treasonable cor-respondence with Austria, but this was buried in an avalanche of false accusations, designed to discredit the monarchy.

The queen was charged with immorality, including the sexual corruption of her son Louis Charles. The prosecution induced a confession from the eight-year-old, and it was decided that the queen should go to the guillotine.

Amid the grief and the counsel against revenge, the heart of Marie Antoinette's farewell letter is an apology for her son's actions. Far from being depraved, she was apparently chaste and

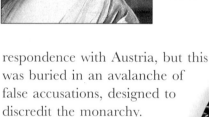

*Above: Marie Antoinette kept this miniature of her son
Louis Charles until her death.*

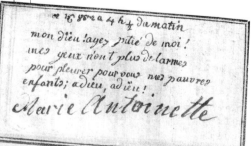

*Left: A last
message: "God
have pity on me!
My eyes have no
more tears to
shed for you my
poor children;
farewell!"*

October 16, 1793

4:30 in the morning

My sister

I am writing to you for the very last time: I have just been condemned to a death that is in no way shameful—since a shameful death is a fate reserved for criminals—but I am going on a journey to meet your brother once again. I hope I will show the same fortitude as he in my last moments.

I am calm, as one always is when one's conscience is clear. I am deeply saddened to abandon my children: you know that I have lived for them alone, as well as for you, my dear and gentle sister, who through your friendship have given everything to be with me.

Where can we find more affection than in the bosom of our families? May my son never forget the dying words of his father, which I have expressly repeated to him: "Never seek to avenge our death."

I have told you things that weigh heavily on my heart. I know how much trouble this boy must cause you: forgive him, my dear sister; remember his youth and how easy it is to speak to a child, yet how hard it is for him to understand you. The day will come, I trust, when he will feel only the worth of your love for the two of them.

Farewell, my good and dear sister; may this letter find its way to you! Think always of me; I embrace you with all my heart, you and my poor, dear children—my God, it is heart-wrenching to leave them for ever! Farewell, farewell! I will now give myself up to my spiritual preparation.

MARIE ANTOINETTE

Above: Marie Antoinette's necklace with medallions holding locks of hair from each of her four children.

Right: Marie Antoinette being led to the guillotine.

sexually timid; Louis had not consummated his marriage with her for seven years. Yet Marie Antoinette knew that it was the sexual charges brought by the prosecution, reinforced by her son's unproven confession, that had condemned her more surely than any of the evidence that she had plotted with foreigners against the revolution.

THOMAS ALVA EDISON
— TO —
HIS PARENTS

October 30, 1870

*The successful inventor sends news
to his parents of his developing career
in New Jersey.*

*Thomas Edison, who defined genius as "one percent
inspiration, ninety-nine percent perspiration."*

Thomas Edison, the seventh and last child in his family, was spoiled by his mother and brutalized by his father. He received only three months of formal education: at age seven, when Thomas's incessant questions drove his teacher to label him "addled," his mother removed him from school and thereafter taught him herself. Thomas's father—who did not understand his son's talents and failed to recognize the inventive genius that would eventually lead Thomas to hold a world-record 1,093 patents—took little part in shaping his inquisitive mind.

By age 16 Thomas was an experienced telegraph operator and soon had his own experimental workshop in Boston. His first invention, patented in 1868, was a vote-recording machine. It taught him the iron law of money when the machine failed to find a market. His next venture was more lucrative. With two business partners, he developed a sophisticated version of a primi-

*Left: Edison's electric
pen created a master
copy that could be
duplicated using a
roller and ink pad.*

tive printing telegraph, called a stock ticker because of the sound it made, and sold his first to Western Union in 1869. He and his partners grossed $5,000 on the sale.

The following year, working for General Marshall Lefferts, president of the Gold and Stock Telegraph Company, he devised an even more complex stock ticker. When Lefferts asked how much he thought the various patents on the invention were worth, Edison thought of naming $5,000 again as the price, but feared he would be thought too greedy; so he parried with: "General, suppose you make me an offer."

Biography

Thomas Edison (1847–1931), born in Milan, Ohio, became a railroad newsboy at the age of 12 and began his experiments in chemistry. A stationmaster taught him telegraphy; Edison proceeded to invent an automatic repeater, by which messages could be sent from one wire to another without an operator. By the early 1870's he was making rapid strides in duplex telegraphy and the printing telegraph. Based in New Jersey, he lengthened the list of his inventions to include quadruplex and sextuplex telegraphy systems, the electric lightbulb and power, the phonograph, kinetoscopes, and storage batteries, establishing himself as one of the greatest inventors of history.

Newark, N.J., Oct. 30 1870
Dear Father and Mother,

Why don't you write to me and tell me the news — you spoke in your last letter that you had a good chance to buy a good piece of property very cheap — if you have your eye on it still, write me describing it, and why you think it valuable. I can send you the money for it. How is mother getting along. You wrote last time she was getting along nicely. I am in a position now to let you have some cash, so you can write and say how much. I may be home sometime this winter. Can't say when exactly for I have a large amount of business to attend to. I have one shop which employs 18 men and am fitting up another which will employ over 150 men — I am now what "you" Democrats call a "Bloated Eastern Manufacturer." Do the Buchanans still live in Port Huron, and is Carrie married yet? Give my love to all.
Your son

To Edison's stupefaction Lefferts replied: "How would $40,000 strike you?" Edison accepted eagerly and was given a check. He knew nothing about banking when he wandered into a Wall Street branch to present the check. His deafness (Edison began to lose his hearing at age 12) prevented him from understanding the instructions the teller gave him, and he had to return to Lefferts's office for advice. Because Edison did not trust the system of bank accounts, he insisted on receiving his payment in a huge wad of 10- and 20-dollar bills, then sat up all night guarding his hoard. His friends finally talked him into opening and using a bank account.

With this princely sum Edison set up his own laboratory and small factory for the commercial production of stock tickers; within 30 days he had spent almost the entire sum he had been paid by Lefferts on equipment for his venture.

However, he felt confident about future prospects and had enough money left over to write this letter to his parents offering to do what he could for them. He particularly wanted "the woman who was the making of me" (as he was to refer to her later) to know of his triumph, and to assure her of financial support. His mother, already very ill, died the following April.

Left: Edison's light bulb burned for more than 40 hours. His earlier attempts to harness electricity for lighting had already cost $40,000.

WILLIAM RANDOLPH HEARST
TO
GEORGE HEARST

1885

*The Harvard student
urges his father to let him reform
the San Francisco Examiner.*

*William Randolph
Hearst, the press
magnate who was
reputed "never to let
the facts interfere
with a good story."*

*George Hearst, who
amassed millions
from ranching and
mining, and
represented California
as a U.S. senator
from 1886 to 1891.*

William Randolph Hearst was a 22-year-old Harvard student when, in 1885, he wrote to his father asking that he be given the *San Francisco Examiner*. As managing editor of Harvard's *Lampoon*, Will Hearst had recently turned this failing journal into a success; in so doing, he became fascinated by journalism.

The *Examiner*, bought in 1880 by the elder Hearst, was the worst newspaper in San Francisco. Its circulation was low, its advertising meager, and its journalism poor; it was also steadily losing money. George Hearst felt understandably reluctant about entrusting it to a novice. But Will's mother exercised her influence on Will's behalf—on one condition: he must agree not to marry the "unsuitable" Eleanor Calhoun. Will agreed to the deal, never forgiving his mother for the hard bargain she had driven.

Will tried to persuade the editor of the *New York Herald*, Ballard Smith, to take the editorship of the *Examiner*. Smith declined and advised Hearst to do the job himself. He did, and began at once to make an indelible mark on journalism.

Perhaps nothing better illustrates the point of view that would contribute to his newspaper fame than the telegram he supposedly sent to an artist when trying to generate popular support for the Spanish-American War in 1898: "You furnish the pictures and I'll furnish the war."

Above: Hearst went from wealth to opulence, living in legendary splendor at San Simeon Castle, California.

Left: Hearst caricatured as a scarecrow in a slough of sensationalism, when he was running for the New York governorship.

Biography

William Randolph Hearst (1863–1951) was the very model of a late 19th-century capitalist. He inherited millions and made more millions. Proprietor of the *San Francisco Examiner* from 1887, he took over the *New York Journal* in 1895 and trebled its circulation. He went on to own over 40 newspapers and magazines. Politicians and industrialists trembled at his word; yet he said toward the end of his life that after acquiring the *Examiner*, "nothing else has ever seemed important."

for our little paper — a tenderness like
y or deformed offspring. I should hate to
nobly for its existence. To tell the
h at some time or other besets most
ccessfully.

Examiner — with enough money to
will do. In the first place I would
make several wide columns where
ve the type spaced more, and these
eater appearance. It would be
. Clip only when absolutely
nece the New York World which
is un the Examiner
shoul people and which
depend enterprise, energy and a certain
startlin originality, and not upon the wisdom of its political
opinions, nor the lofty style of its editorials.

To accomplish this we must have — as the World
has — active, intelligent and energetic young men. We must
have men who come out West in the hopeful buoyancy of
youth for the purpose of making their fortune, and not a
worthless scum that have been carried there by the eddies
of repeated failures.

Another detail of unquestionable importance is that
we actually or apparently establish some connection between
ourselves and the New York World, and obtain a certain prestige in bearing
some relation to that paper.

And now is the most important suggestion — all these changes should not
be made by degrees, but at once so that the improvement will be very marked and
noticeable and will attract universal attention and comment.

WILL

VIRGINIA STEPHEN
TO
LEONARD WOOLF

May 1, 1912

*The talented and beautiful young writer
replies, with devastating honesty,
to her future husband's proposal of marriage.*

*Virginia Stephen Woolf, an
innovator of modern fiction,
who was educated at home.*

irginia Stephen and her elder sister, Vanessa, were described by Leonard Woolf as "young women of astonishing beauty . . . . It was almost impossible for a man not to fall in love with them." Leonard himself developed a deep attraction to Virginia while on a long leave in London in 1911, after seven years in the civil service in Ceylon (now Sri Lanka).

Upon the death of her father in 1904, Virginia had left her family's upper-middle-class world in London's staid Kensington to live and write in bohemian Bloomsbury. Leonard and Virginia developed an easy companionship that continued to grow after he joined her shared house. After his first proposal, in January 1912, Leonard resigned from the

*Left: The cover of this
edition of* To the
Lighthouse *was
painted by Vanessa Bell,
Virginia's sister.*

civil service to avoid going back to Ceylon, in the hope that Virginia would accept his marriage proposal.

Virginia had mixed feelings about marriage and resented the role prescribed for women in British society. She was also repelled by the idea of sex with a man, after the trauma of a childhood in which she was molested by her two older half-brothers. As an adult Virginia's most intense emotional relationships were with women. Nevertheless, she wrote of Leonard in May 1912: "I've known him only 6 months, but from the first I have found him the one person to talk to." Leonard seemed content to be loved in this way and loved Virginia for her intellectual prowess.

Biography

Virginia Woolf (1882–1941) was one of the great innovators of 20th-century fiction. She finished her first novel, *The Voyage Out*, at the age of 24, though it was not published until she was 33. Her subsequent work included *Night and Day* (1919), *Mrs. Dalloway* (1925), *To the Lighthouse* (1927), *Orlando* (1928), *The Waves* (1931), and *The Years* (1937). Her style was experimental and impressionistic, and several of her novels explored women's dilemmas. She was also a distinguished essayist and critic, and in 1917 she founded the Hogarth Press with her husband. Achievement and success notwithstanding, Virginia suffered all her life from bouts of mental illness, and ultimately took her own life.

Dearest Leonard,

To deal with the facts first (my fingers are so cold I can hardly write) I shall be back about 7 tomorrow, so there will be time to discuss — but what does it mean? You can't take the leave, I suppose, if you are going to resign certainly at the end of it. Anyhow, it shows what a career you're ruining!

Well then, as to all the rest. It seems to me that I am giving you a great deal of pain — some in the most casual way — & therefore I ought to be as plain with you as I can. Of course I can't explain what I feel — these are some of the things that strike me. The obvious advantages of marriage stand in my way. . . . I will not look upon marriage as a profession. . . . Then, of course, I feel angry sometimes at the strength of your desire. . . . And then I am fearfully unstable. . . . I pass from hot to cold in an instant, without any reason . . . in spite of these feelings, which go chasing each other all day long, when I am with you, there is some feeling which is permanent, and growing. You want to know of course whether it will ever make me marry you. How can I say? I think it will. . . . But I don't know what the future will bring. I'm half afraid of myself. . . . I sometimes think that if I married you, I could have everything — & then — is it the sexual side of it that comes between us? As I told you brutally the other day, I feel no physical attraction in you. . . . But you have made me very happy too. We both of us want a marriage that is a tremendous living thing, always alive, always hot, not dead and easy in parts as most marriages are. We ask a great deal of life, don't we? Perhaps we shall get it; then, how splendid!

Yrs

V. S.

Virginia's letter to Leonard (abstracted above) expressed reservations that would have made many men withdraw their proposal. But after more painfully honest discussion, the two were married on August 10 at a registry office in London. Over the next 30 years of an unconsummated marriage, Leonard provided a stable but stimulating environment to nurture his wife's literary talent and bolster her frail mental health.

Right: "Conversation Piece" by Vanessa Bell (1912). The figures have been identified as Adrian Stephen (the artist's younger brother), Leonard Woolf, and Clive Bell.

BARTOLOMEO VANZETTI
TO
DANTE SACCO

August 21, 1927

*The unjustly condemned anarchist
writes to his friend's son
shortly before their execution.*

*Sacco and Vanzetti in court, one of a series of paintings
by Ben Shahn (1898–1969).*

The notorious case of Sacco and Vanzetti exemplifies the "reds under the bed" hysteria that swept through the United States in the years immediately after World War I. Paranoia about communist subversion after the Russian Revolution of 1917 led to thousands of foreign suspects being deported. It was in this xenophobic atmosphere that the authorities in Massachusetts determined to bring to justice the gang responsible for two armed robberies that occurred in the winter and spring of 1919–20. During the second robbery two men had been killed; the hunt for the killers centered on "Italians" that eyewitnesses claimed to have seen.

Nicola Sacco and Bartolomeo Vanzetti were arrested, found guilty by a jury that included no Italian-Americans, and sentenced to death. Sacco was a factory worker with a solid alibi based on his time card and the testimony of his workmates. Vanzetti had that of his customers, many of whom remembered buying fish from him when he was supposed to be committing the crime.

This patently questionable conviction brought, first, a national outcry by liberal opinion and, later, an international protest movement. Yet

Left: British sympathizers advertise a rally in London's Hyde Park (1927).

SAVE SACCO & VANZETTI
PROTEST DEMONSTRATION AGAINST DEATH SENTENCE
HYDE PARK WEDNESDAY 10 AT 7 PM
COME IN YOUR THOUSANDS

Biography

Nicola Sacco (1891–1927) and Bartolomeo Vanzetti (1888–1927), Italian-born immigrants, a shoemaker and a fish peddler, were the principals in an American *cause célèbre* in the 1920's that has become a byword for injustice. In 1920, after a trial in which the judge was influenced by prejudice against the defendants' political anarchism, Sacco and Vanzetti were convicted of a payroll murder and robbery in Boston. Alibis, inconsistency in the prosecution's case, and even a convincing confession to the crime by another prisoner in 1925 did not move the Massachusetts authorities, and after seven years of appeals the two were executed in the electric chair.

My Dear Dante:

I still hope, and we will fight until the last moment, to revindicate our right to live and to be free, but all the forces of the State and of the money and reaction are deadly against us because we are libertarians or anarchists.

I tell you now that all that I know of your father, he is not a criminal, but one of the bravest men I ever knew. Some day you will understand what I am about to tell you. That your father has sacrificed everything dear and sacred to the human heart and soul for his fate in liberty and justice for all.

That day you will be proud of your father, and if you come brave enough, you will take his place in the struggle between tyranny and liberty and you will vindicate his (our) names and our blood.

Remember, Dante, remember always these things; we are not criminals; they convicted us on a frame-up; they denied us a new trial; and if we will be executed after seven years, four months and seventeen days of unspeakable tortures and wrong, it is for what I have already told you; because we were for the poor and against the exploitation and oppression of the man by the man.

The day will come when you will understand the atrocious cause of the above written words, in all its fullness. Then you will honor us.

Now Dante, be brave and good always. I embrace you.

Bartolomeo Vanzetti.

Judge Webster Thayer, backed by the U.S. Supreme Court, upheld the sentence and rejected every attempt to secure a retrial.

When they were arrested, Sacco and Vanzetti barely spoke English. While they languished in prison as the efforts to save them dragged on for seven years of appeals, they improved their English considerably, and Vanzetti, in the farewell letter to Sacco's son extracted here, became eloquent in courageous despair. On hearing that the death sentence would be carried out in the electric chair, Vanzetti wrote: "That last moment belongs to us—that agony is our triumph."

Above: The funeral procession, after Sacco and Vanzetti were executed, on August 23, 1927.

POLICY
&
CHALLENGES

Whereas a private letter will sometimes display the writer's most honest thoughts, a letter on public matters, written to advise, encourage, or challenge its recipient, will probably conceal, as much as reveal, the innermost feelings of the sender. In a vast and far-flung organization, such as the Roman empire at its height, the exchange of letters between the emperor and administrators of distant provinces provided a crucial lifeline of authority and decision making. Yet even with a special courier service traveling on the excellent roads of the empire at a rate of 50 miles a day, the news might be weeks out of date by the time it arrived. In Manchu China, couriers from Beijing received mandated limits on how long they could take to reach the outposts of empire (two weeks to reach Shanghai, six weeks for the farthest, southerly, regions). In such circumstances the correspondence between the central authority and provincial governors, who often sought maximum freedom of action, tended to be deliberately obscure. In this regard, Pliny's honesty in writing for advice on how to administer imperial policy on the tricky question of an outlawed but apparently harmless sect is unusual. The Apostle Paul's epistles, letters to the nascent Christian churches of Asia Minor and Greece written some 60 years prior to Pliny's, display a similar use of the letter to establish authority—in this case to steer the policies and beliefs of a widespread flock. The dangers implicit in such a means of communication are noted by Joan of Arc, 1400 years later, when writing to the people of Reims to bolster their morale. She dared not tell her news for fear that the letter might fall into the hands of the enemy. The threat that a message might be lost by capture of the messenger was lessened with the advent of printing, and the consequent development of the published open letter. Émile Zola's missive ("I accuse") to the French president is one of the best-known examples in history.

Political action, though, often includes personal manipulation, and letters on political matters may contain encouragements or discouragements for their recipients—some more overt than others. Lorenzo de' Medici, writing to his son Giovanni, shortly to become pope, with sound advice on suitable behavior, also ensured his own grasp on political power in Renaissance Italy. Napoleon, curtly dismissing Louis XVIII, the Bourbon claimant to the French throne in 1799, asserted once and for all his commitment to the values of the Revolution; and Neville Chamberlain, summing up his discussions with Hitler over the future of Czechoslovakia, seemed to signal, intentionally or otherwise, his acquiescence in German aggression.

More deliberately coded were the instructions from Sir Francis Walsingham, Elizabeth I's secretary of state, permitting Francis Drake to prey on Spanish shipping. By comparison, the putdown by Louis XIV of his minister, Colbert, was a masterpiece of directness from a man said to find face-to-face confrontation very difficult. All of these letters reveal, and conceal, different aspects of the truth in service to the politics, ambitions, and motivations of each sender.

SAINT PAUL
TO
THE CORINTHIANS

A.D. 54

*The Apostle Paul offers guidance to
the people of Corinth on Christian morality
and brotherly love.*

An ivory relief from 4th-century Italy, representing any of the apostles.

This letter is one of the great classics of letter-writing, adopted as a book within the New Testament—an epistle. Written at Ephesus (in modern Turkey) and sent to Corinth in Greece in A.D. 54, it contains some of the apostle's best-known phrases: "It is better to marry than to burn," "For now we see through a glass, darkly," and "O death, where is thy sting?" The core exhortation of Paul's letter is that people should love their fellow beings; he uses the Greek word *agape* (translated as "charity" in the Authorized Version of the Bible), which means universal, as opposed to erotic, love.

Born Saul of Tarsus, a Pharisee and also a Roman citizen, he never met Jesus but he did persecute Christians, whom he considered apostate Jews. After experiencing a vision of Christ on the road to Damascus, however, he became their champion. From then on, Saul became known as Paul.

In taking the gospel of Jesus to the Gentiles (non-Jews) and proclaiming the divinity of Jesus as the Christ, Paul played a major part in ensuring that Christianity would become a universal religion. For nearly 30 years, Paul journeyed throughout the eastern Mediterranean, establishing colonies ("churches") of Christians and enduring many hardships. As he told the Corinthians in his second letter: "Five times the Jews have given me the thirty-nine strokes; three times I have been beaten with rods; once I was stoned; three times I have been shipwrecked, and for twenty-four hours I was adrift on the open sea."

Bread stamps used by the early Christians to imprint the staff of life with sacred messages.

From Paul, apostle of Jesus Christ at God's call and by God's will together with our colleague Sosthenes, to the congregation of God's people at Corinth, dedicated to him in Christ Jesus, . . . Grace and peace to you from God our Father and the Lord Jesus Christ.

. . . . The higher gifts are those you should aim at.

And now I will show you the best way of all.

I may speak in tongues of men or of angels, but if I am without love, I am a sounding gong or a clanging cymbal. I may have the gift of prophecy, and know every hidden truth; I may have faith strong enough to move mountains; but if I have no love, I am nothing. I may dole out all I possess, or even give my body to be burned, but if I have no love, I am none the better.

Love is patient; love is kind and envies no one. Love is never boastful, nor conceited, nor rude; never selfish, not quick to take offense. Love keeps no score of wrongs; does not gloat over other men's sins, but delights in the truth. There is nothing love cannot face; there is no limit to its faith, its hope, and its endurance.

. . . . Greetings from the congregation in Asia. Many greetings in the Lord from Aquila and Prisca and the congregation at their house. Greetings from all the brothers. Greet one another with the kiss of peace.

This greeting is in my own hand

PAUL

(Extract from New English Bible)

Paul preached that the old Jewish Law was no longer binding and that salvation was attainable solely because of Christ's crucifixion and resurrection. Many Christian converts assumed that faith alone was enough and that in other respects they could behave as they pleased. The purpose of Paul's first letter to Corinth was to lay down guidelines. His great hymn of praise to love formed the heart of Paul's pastoral advice, but he also warned against religious factionalism, eating sacrificial meat, sexual immorality, and women participating in religious meetings. This has led to the accusation that Paul was a misogynist, but given the ancient Jewish attitudes, he showed a measure of tolerance toward women.

Above: Arms raised in worship, this sixth-century figure adopts an attitude of prayer commonly used by early Christians.

Left: The Temple of Apollo, Corinth, built between 560 and 550 B.C.

PLINY THE YOUNGER
TO
EMPEROR TRAJAN

A.D. 112

*An imperial administrator seeks
the right way to deal with members of
a religious cult—the Christians.*

*Pliny the Younger,
whose letters
provide a mine of
information on
Roman life in the
first century.*

*Trajan, an
excellent
administrator
and leader, who
ruled from
98–117.*

f all history's surviving letters, this one has clear claims to being among the most valuable as historical evidence, for it, and the reply it drew from Trajan, contain the earliest and fullest accounts of Roman conflict with Christians during their first hundred years of existence.

One of the truly gifted letter writers of history, Gaius Plinius Secundus (usually known as Pliny the Younger to distinguish him from his uncle of the same name) is a prime source of knowledge about the life of the Roman upper class in the first century. He had a brilliant career in law and administration, culminating in his appointment by the Emperor Trajan in 110 as governor in the province of Bithynia and Pontus (present-day northern Turkey).

Trajan appointed Pliny because of his recognized expertise in finance and his familiarity with local affairs. That the province was wracked by political disorder, administrative mismanagement, and municipal corruption apparently did not come as a surprise to Pliny, but he did not expect a deluge of complaints against the Christians. The Greek population of Bithynia and Pontus particularly disliked them because they did not integrate sufficiently with the wider community. Pliny's letter provides the earliest non-Christian reference to the services of the early church. Translated in an abridged form here, the letter also reveals what careful observance Roman law demanded. Pliny's own close observance of legal forms comes through in his sending Roman citizens to Rome for judgment and his separate treatment of accused persons

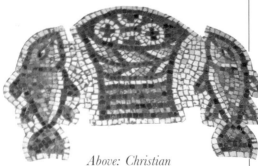

*Above: Christian
symbols from the first
century—the miracle of the
bread and the fishes in a
mosaic floor.*

Biography

Pliny the Younger (about A.D. 62–113) was born into a wealthy landowning family in northern Italy. He wrote a Greek tragedy at the age of 14 and by the time he was 18 years old was so skilled an orator that he could plead cases in the Forum in Rome. At the earliest permissible age he held all the high offices in Roman administration and under Emperor Domitian headed the military treasury and senatorial treasury. He died in office as imperial administrator in Bithynia and Pontus. Pliny was a generous, hospitable and—by the standards of the time—humane man. He married three times; his letters contain many memories of his beloved third wife, Calpurnia.

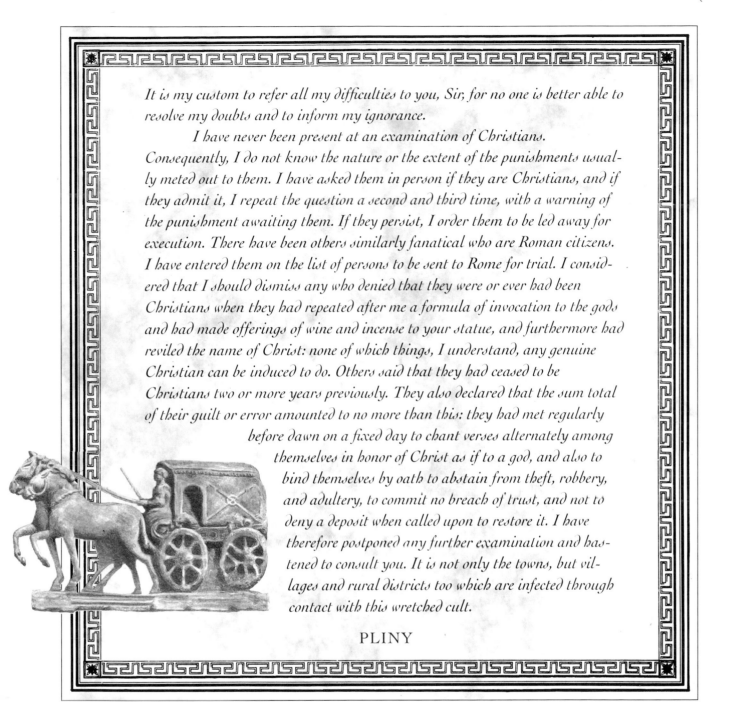

It is my custom to refer all my difficulties to you, Sir, for no one is better able to resolve my doubts and to inform my ignorance.

I have never been present at an examination of Christians. Consequently, I do not know the nature or the extent of the punishments usually meted out to them. I have asked them in person if they are Christians, and if they admit it, I repeat the question a second and third time, with a warning of the punishment awaiting them. If they persist, I order them to be led away for execution. There have been others similarly fanatical who are Roman citizens. I have entered them on the list of persons to be sent to Rome for trial. I considered that I should dismiss any who denied that they were or ever had been Christians when they had repeated after me a formula of invocation to the gods and had made offerings of wine and incense to your statue, and furthermore had reviled the name of Christ: none of which things, I understand, any genuine Christian can be induced to do. Others said that they had ceased to be Christians two or more years previously. They also declared that the sum total of their guilt or error amounted to no more than this: they had met regularly before dawn on a fixed day to chant verses alternately among themselves in honor of Christ as if to a god, and also to bind themselves by oath to abstain from theft, robbery, and adultery, to commit no breach of trust, and not to deny a deposit when called upon to restore it. I have therefore postponed any further examination and hastened to consult you. It is not only the towns, but villages and rural districts too which are infected through contact with this wretched cult.

PLINY

who admitted to being Christians and those who did not. The test of sacrificing to the Emperor's image with wine and incense was given to those who denied being Christians; only later in the history of the empire would governors try to force Christians to sacrifice. And only Nero among the early emperors actively persecuted them.

In his reply, Trajan advised Pliny to follow local custom, insisting on Christian obedience to the law as a matter of principle, but avoiding persecution. Some later emperors tended to use Trajan's ruling as a precedent; his moderate answer to Pliny helped to limit the scale and frequency of persecutions against Christians.

Above left: A wagon and horses like the ones that would have carried official dispatches to Trajan.

Right: Pagan symbols from the first century—a sacrificial bull and a knife for sacrificial killing.

Joan of Arc
to
The People of Reims

March 16, 1430

Joan the Maid writes to offer encouragement, support, and reassurance to the people of a town under threat of attack.

Reputedly a good likeness, this miniature was made 20 years after Joan was burned.

 his letter was composed by Joan of Arc at the peak of her success. As a result of her truly extraordinary achievements the year before, Joan's name had a charismatic pull for the people of France in March 1430. Inspired by "voices" ordering her to save France, she had persuaded the local commander to take her across English-occupied territory to meet the dauphin, the weak and ugly son of the lunatic Charles VI. The dauphin clung to his claim to the French throne even though the English controlled northern France and had proclaimed Henry VI king of both England and France.

Biography

Saint Joan of Arc, (about 1412–31), French patriot and Christian martyr, was born the daughter of well-off peasants at Domrémy, a hamlet on the borders of Lorraine and Champagne. In her teens she claimed to hear the voices of Saint Michael, Saint Catherine, and Saint Margaret ordering her to rescue France from English domination. Her leadership was instrumental in raising the siege of Orléans in 1429, but at a similar venture at Compiègne she was captured and sold to the English. The English persuaded a French ecclesiastical court of the Inquisition to try her for heresy and sorcery. She was burned at the stake at Rouen in 1431, and was canonized by the Catholic Church in 1920.

At Joan's first meeting with the dauphin, she spoke to him privately and told him that she knew what he had prayed for. This confirmed both the divine origin of her mission and the legitimacy of his claim to the throne.

Subjected to an ecclesiastical examination at Poitiers, which she passed easily, Joan was allowed to join the army gathering at Blois for the relief of Orléans. Traveling with her own standard and her distinctive suit of white armor, Joan took command of the troops.

On April 29, 1429, Joan entered Orléans, a city that had been under siege since October 12, 1428. By May 8 the English forts that surrounded the city had been captured and the siege of Orléans was broken. The English fell back

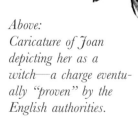

Above: Caricature of Joan depicting her as a witch—a charge eventually "proven" by the English authorities.

Above right: 15th-century pike and crossbow.

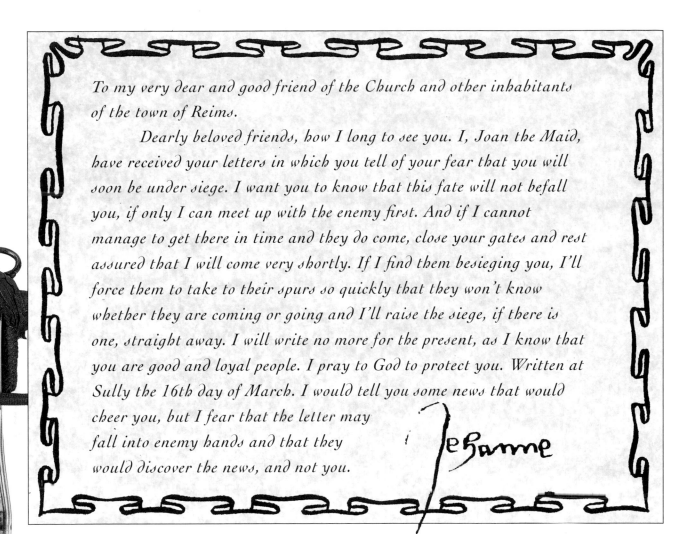

To my very dear and good friend of the Church and other inhabitants of the town of Reims.

Dearly beloved friends, how I long to see you. I, Joan the Maid, have received your letters in which you tell of your fear that you will soon be under siege. I want you to know that this fate will not befall you, if only I can meet up with the enemy first. And if I cannot manage to get there in time and they do come, close your gates and rest assured that I will come very shortly. If I find them besieging you, I'll force them to take to their spurs so quickly that they won't know whether they are coming or going and I'll raise the siege, if there is one, straight away. I will write no more for the present, as I know that you are good and loyal people. I pray to God to protect you. Written at Sully the 16th day of March. I would tell you some news that would cheer you, but I fear that the letter may fall into enemy hands and that they would discover the news, and not you.

Jehanne

in disarray from their principal strongholds on the River Loire. To breathe further courage into French resistance, Joan took the dauphin with an army of 12,000 men through English-held territory to Reims cathedral, where on July 17, 1429, he was crowned Charles VII.

After the coronation, the lackluster Charles ignored Joan's pleas to march on Paris, but allowed Joan to move against it herself. Jealous of her fame, he proceeded to betray her by having his own men destroy her assault bridge. He then entered into a truce with the duke of Burgundy, principal ally of the English. Shortly afterward Charles disbanded the army.

By the time Joan wrote this letter, hostilities had resumed. Joan's inner voices warned her that she had little more than a year left to live, and she worried that the duke of Burgundy was planning a spring offensive. Shortly after writing this

letter, Joan left for Compiègne, now under siege by the Burgundians. The cowardice—or treachery—of Compiègne's mayor led to Joan's capture on June 24, after her army was beaten back.

There followed Joan's protracted trial, the death sentence, her recantation, then reaffirmation of the voices, and finally her martyrdom at Rouen on May 30, 1431. Joan died totally abandoned by the powerful: by Charles (who refused to ransom her); by the English because her leadership brought the French army victory against them in battle; and by the church because its authority was threatened by someone who had claimed direct access to God. Only with the people of France did Joan never lose her popularity.

LORENZO DE' MEDICI
TO
HIS SON GIOVANNI

April, 1492

The Florentine leader sends guidance and advice to his son, as Giovanni embarks on a distinguished career in the church.

Lorenzo the Magnificent, who knew his family needed lasting influence in the papal court.

Giovanni de' Medici, whose appointment as cardinal was kept secret until he reached the age of 16.

 his letter represents an attempt by the greatest of the Medici, Lorenzo the Magnificent, to prolong the power and influence of his family. The Medici, a Florentine family, had amassed their great wealth through the successes of the banker Giovanni (1360–1429). Cosimo his son (1389–1464) then initiated a golden age in the family's history. He brought peace and security to Florence, used his wealth to encourage learning

Above: An idealized Lorenzo as the youngest of the three Magi in a painting by Benozzo Gozzoli (1420–97).

Right: The Medici family crest.

and the arts, and enriched the city with magnificent buildings and libraries, accelerating two momentous forces in Italy: the Renaissance and early capitalism. The Medici genius filled the vacuum left by the decay of feudalism and church power with a political system that rested ultimately on money and the financial clout of the Medici bankers.

Lorenzo was the son of Piero di Cosimo

(1416–69) and grandson of Cosimo. Piero ostensibly ran Florence for five troubled years, but his constant battle with gout made Lorenzo the real power in the family from the age of 16. Old beyond his years when he assumed supreme power at the age of 21, Lorenzo remained officially a private citizen, always careful to play the servant rather than the master of Florence, though no one doubted where the power lay. He ruled justly and magnanimously and was a friend and patron of artists and scholars as well as a promoter of the new technology of printing. A distinguished lyric poet, he also took part in the proceedings of the Platonic Academy. Yet the

Biography

*L*orenzo de' Medici (1449–92) presided over the most glorious period of Florence's history, sometimes called the Laurentian Age (1469–92). He ruled Florence ostensibly using constitutional methods, yet reduced the powers of the popular assemblies in 1471. Though officially a simple citizen, he was recognized as a benevolent tyrant. While his critics alleged that he weakened the forms of government set up by his father, his contribution to the arts in Florence was second to none. He employed his vast wealth to encourage art and literature, made Florence the center of the revival of learning, acted as patron for painters and sculptors, and thus contributed significantly to the Renaissance.

You, and all of us who are interested in your welfare, ought to esteem ourselves highly favored by Providence, not only for the many honors and benefits bestowed on our house, but more particularly for having conferred upon us, in your person, the greatest dignity we have ever enjoyed.

Endeavor therefore to alleviate the burden of your early dignity by the regularity of your life and by your perseverance in those studies which are suitable to your profession. It gave me great satisfaction to learn that, in the course of the past year, you had frequently, of your own accord, gone to communion and confession. The influence of example is itself prevalent; but you will probably meet with those who will particularly endeavor to corrupt and incite you to vice; because, as you may yourself perceive, your early attainment to so great a dignity is not observed without envy, and those who could not prevent your receiving that honor will secretly endeavor to diminish it, by inducing you to forfeit the good estimation of the public. To these difficulties you ought to oppose yourself with the greater firmness, as there is at present less virtue amongst your brethren of the college. I acknowledge indeed that several of them are good and learned men, whose lives are exemplary, and whom I would recommend to you as patterns of your conduct.

With those of less respectable character converse not with too much intimacy; not merely on account of the circumstance itself, but for the sake of public opinion. Converse on general topics with all. On public occasions let your equipage and dress be rather below than above mediocrity. There is one rule which I would recommend to your attention in preference to all others: rise early in the morning. This will not only contribute to your health, but will enable you to arrange and expedite the business of the day. You will probably be desired to intercede for the favors of the Pope on particular occasions. Be cautious, however, that you trouble him not too often; and if you should be obliged to request some kindness from him, let it be done with that modesty and humility which are so pleasing to his disposition.

Farewell.

*Laurentius et
medicis*

Above: Florence around 1480, at the height of its "Laurentian Age"—the time of Lorenzo.

Medici also had many enemies, as became fatally apparent in the Pazzi conspiracy. The Pazzi, another banking family, devised a plot with the backing of Pope Sixtus IV to assassinate Lorenzo and his brother Giuliano on Easter Day 1478. Giuliano was killed during Mass in Florence cathedral. Lorenzo, though wounded, escaped into the sacristy, which had recently been fitted with heavy bronze doors that kept the assassins at bay. The plot's failure and Lorenzo's courage increased his popularity. No one thereafter disputed his authority in Florence.

However, in failing health by the end of the 1480's, he worried about the Medici's future. His elder son Piero seemed unlikely to make an effec-

92

tive head of the family; there was increasing conflict with the papal states; and Lorenzo himself had not proven a particularly successful businessman.

Lorenzo believed that to assure their future, the family would need friends at the papal court. He laid his plans cautiously. The first step came in 1483 when the king of France agreed to give an abbey to Lorenzo's son, Giovanni, then seven years old. Marriage between the pope's son (born before his father joined the church) and Lorenzo's daughter helped close the distance to Rome. In March 1489 Giovanni, aged 13, received his cardinal's hat and three other rich abbeys as income. Although it was not unusual at this time to make mere boys into cardinals, the pope insisted that the cardinalate be kept secret until Giovanni was 16.

On March 9, 1492, of the proper age, Giovanni officially became a member of the Sacred College of Cardinals in a ceremony of great splendor, held in Fiesole on the hill overlooking Florence. Lorenzo was too ill to attend, but before the ceremony he saw his son briefly for the last time. He then sent him the letter extracted here, to advise him against the dangers he would encounter in Rome.

Lorenzo's misgivings about his eldest son Piero were well founded. Immediately after his father's death, Piero de' Medici (1472–1503) allied himself with the king of Naples against Lodovico Sforza of Milan; Sforza in turn called to his aid Charles VIII of France, with the result that Piero was forced to surrender Pisa and Livorno to the French. Incensed at his cowardice, the Florentines drove Piero from the city and declared the Medici traitors

Above and right: Lending made the Medicis rich and the gold florin Europe's most stable currency.

Below: A Medici account book and quill for recording debts.

and rebels. All efforts of the Medici to regain their powers failed until 1512, when a Spanish papal army invaded Tuscany, the town of Prato was sacked, and the people of Florence were forced to recall the Medici, headed by Piero's brother Giuliano (1479–1516).

Giovanni (1475–1521) meanwhile distinguished himself in the College of Cardinals and was employed as legate by the warrior-pope Julius II. He earned a reputation for piety and strict propriety. On Julius's death, he was elected pope as Leo X. His achievements were many: he signed a concordat with Francis I of France; he brought the fifth Lateran Council to a successful conclusion; he consolidated and extended Julius II's conquests; and he made himself a notable patron of learning and the arts. As part of a vast project for rebuilding St. Peter's he allowed the sale of indulgences, a decision destined to trigger Luther's rebellion and hence the Reformation. Giovanni's power and influence enabled Cosimo de' Medici (1519–74), "the Great," to reestablish a Medici dynasty in Tuscany, which would endure into the 18th century.

SIR FRANCIS WALSINGHAM
TO
FRANCIS DRAKE

1577

*The Elizabethan courtier's instructions send
Drake on a voyage of exploration that is unofficial,
but authorized, piracy.*

*Walsingham, an
uncompromising
Protestant who
wanted to
undermine the
Catholic kings.*

*Drake, whose
secret orders left
him personally
responsible for
his actions.*

 n 1577 the English mariner Francis Drake was summoned to London to meet Francis Walsingham, the secretary of state. Walsingham proposed that Drake undertake a trading mission to South America on behalf of a syndicate of powerful courtiers, including himself.

In the summer of the same year Walsingham sent Drake a letter of instruction (reproduced here with large gaps due to damage by fire). The letter directed him to pass through the Strait of Magellan and explore the continental coast beyond (which comprises modern Chile). He was to discover places where English goods could be sold and to prospect for precious metals. At the same time, he should make friends with the "lords" of those countries, bestowing on them gifts to the value of £50. After five months on the Pacific coast, Drake was then to return by the Strait of Magellan. The whole voyage was to last 13 months.

In reality Drake spent three years circumnavigating the globe, and much of that time was devoted to devastating Spanish colonies on the Pacific coast of South America. Why was his actual voyage so different from the instructions given in the letter?

Drake later revealed what had happened. Summoned into the presence of the queen, Elizabeth I, he received secret instructions to prey on Spanish colonies on the

*Drake's fold-up
navigational
instruments.*

Biography

Sir Francis Walsingham (about 1532–90) was the son of a lawyer and began his own career in law in 1552. In 1563 he obtained his first seat in Parliament. He was ambassador to the French court in 1570–73, admitted to the Privy Council, and appointed secretary of state in December 1573, a post he held until his death. A vigilant secretary, he spent much time detecting and thwarting Catholic conspiracies against the queen. His skill as a diplomat made him valuable in carrying out Elizabeth I's foreign policy, which he loyally pursued even when she went against his advice. He was knighted in 1577, and subsequently made chancellor of the Order of the Garter.

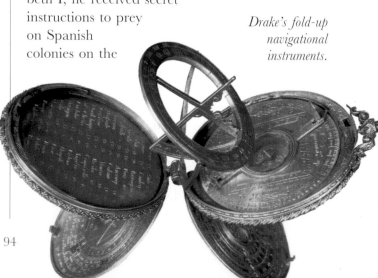

... as of the other to find out ... to have traffic for the vent of Her Majesty's realms. They are not under the obedience of princes, so is there great hope of spices, drugs, cochineal, and special commodities, such as may extend Her Highness's dominions, and also ... shipping a-work greatly and ... gotten up as aforesaid into 30 degrees ... the South Sea (if it shall be thought ... by the forenamed Francis Drake ... to ... far) then he is to return the same way homewards as he went out, which voyage by God's favor is to be performed in 12 month. Although he should spend 5 months in tarrying upon the coast to get knowle[dge] of the princes and countries there.

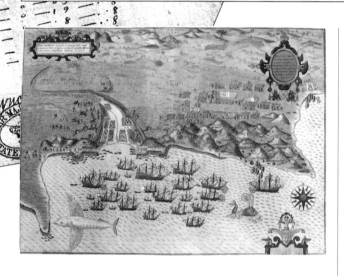

Top left: An inventory of the treasure Drake brought back.

Left: A Spanish portrayal of Drake's attack on their colony at Santiago, Hispaniola.

Below: One of Drake's banners.

Pacific coast of South America. "Drake," said the queen, "so it is that I would gladly be revenged on the king of Spain for divers injuries that I have received." She told him that the only way to strike effectively at Philip II, the Catholic king of Spain, was in the Americas, the source of his wealth (in the form of silver bullion). Furthermore, Drake was the only man who could carry out the mission. However, if the plan miscarried or Drake was captured, she would deny all knowledge of his activities. Drake's sack and pillage of Spanish settlements during the voyage of 1577–80 was therefore a clear act of piracy under international law. For Drake to be within the law, it was necessary either that England and Spain should be at war or that he should carry a letter from the queen authorizing him to prey on Spanish shipping in retaliation for past English losses. The difference between a licensed privateer and a pirate rested on these letters of authorization, called letters of marque. Without one, a ship engaged in hostilities was operating outside the law of nations and was, therefore, a pirate.

The queen dared not commission Drake overtly—this would have been tantamount to a declaration of war on Spain. Had Drake been caught, the English government could have pointed to the letter of instruction and claimed that Drake had exceeded his authority. Drake might have been executed as a pirate, but he survived to be honored by the queen who had put him at such risk.

LOUIS XIV
— TO —
JEAN-BAPTISTE COLBERT

April 24, 1671

The "Sun King" issues a stern warning to his controller-general not to risk challenging the will of the king.

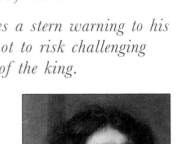

Louis XIV, who became more and more despotic as his long reign continued.

Jean-Baptiste Colbert, the first administrator to give serious attention to the French navy.

n 1661, after 18 years as a boy king dominated by powerful ministers, Louis XIV decided that he and he alone, at 23, would rule France; *L'état c'est moi* ("I am the state") became his watchword. He worked nine hours a day on affairs of state, packed the councils of state with his own handpicked men, and insisted that every piece of legislative, diplomatic, or fiscal business bear his signature. He issued *lettres de cachet* (unappealable notifications of banishment) to anyone who displeased him—more than 9,000 of them over the course of his long reign. Obsessed by autocratic power, he allowed no opposition or criticism.

Biography

Louis XIV (1638–1715), known as the "Sun King," came to the throne at the age of 4, but had no power until 1661, when Cardinal Mazarin, who had effectively ruled during the period of regency, died. He then became the essence of absolute monarchy, and proceeded to use up France's wealth in 50 years of frequent warfare. His narrow religious stance led to the persecution of French Protestants, the Huguenots—including the revocation of the Edict of Nantes in 1685. For political reasons, in 1660 he married Marie-Thérèse of Austria, daughter of the king of Spain; she died in 1683. After her death Louis secretly married Madame de Maintenon, the third of his famous mistresses.

Louis's most able minister, the recipient of this letter, was Jean-Baptiste Colbert (1619–83). Formerly assistant to Cardinal Mazarin, Colbert had brought about the downfall of the finance minister, Fouquet, in 1661. He himself then quickly rose to the supreme position of political power under Louis XIV— the controller-general of finances. Colbert worked harder than the king, spending up to 16 hours a day at his desk. A great administrator and financial reformer, he put French finances on a sound footing, built up the navy, and fostered French colonialism. He also amassed a huge personal fortune.

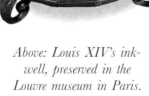

Above: Louis XIV's inkwell, preserved in the Louvre museum in Paris.

Colbert's greatest love, the French navy, brought him into temporary conflict with the king. Colbert wanted to build the most powerful fleet in the world. His desire to spend revenues on even more warships rather than on the extravagance of Louis's great

Chantilly, 24th April 1671

The day before yesterday I was master of myself sufficiently to hide from you the grief that I suffered in listening to a man on whom I have showered benefits talking to me in the way that you did on that occasion.

I have always had a great affection for you, and from my actions it seems evident that I still have. I believe that I am giving a great indication of this by telling you that I restrained myself for a moment, not wanting to say to your face the things I am now writing to you, so that you could not offend me further. It is the memory of the services you have done for me and my friendship for you that make me approach you thus; take advantage of them and don't make the mistake of distressing me further, for after I have heard your reasons and those of your associates, and when I have pronounced judgment on all your pretensions, I don't ever want to speak of the subject again.

See whether the navy is suitable for you, if you don't have it as you want, or if you would prefer something different. Speak freely. But after I give you a decision, I don't want to hear any more on the matter.

I am telling you exactly what I think so that you can work from a secure foundation and do not take false steps.

new palace at Versailles prompted this chilling letter—a clear signal of what happened to those who dared to oppose the will of the king.

Colbert knew that, despite his power and talents, to persist would mean a *lettre de cachet*, or perhaps even lifetime imprisonment. Louis XIV disliked face-to-face confrontation; but he was vindictive and unforgiving if his ministers did not immediately bow to his will. The prudent Colbert never again made the mistake of risking the king's disfavor, and remained in his post until his death in 1681, albeit bitter about the king's excesses and hated by the people for his punitive taxes. His drive to make France great in every sphere of life was thwarted, before and after his death, by the zest for war of the king and his war minister, Louvois. Despite Colbert's best efforts, when Louis XIV died in 1715, France was bankrupt.

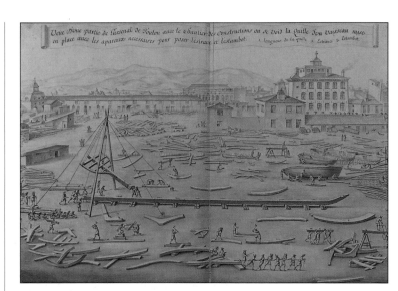

Above: This view of the ship-building yards he created in the arsenal at Marseilles was drawn for Colbert's official records of naval developments.

NAPOLEON BONAPARTE
TO
LOUIS XVIII

1800

*The first consul of France warns
the executed king's brother never
to return to his country.*

*Napoleon Bonaparte,
who rose from sub-
lieutenant of artillery
to become emperor of
the French.*

*Louis XVIII, who
eventually reigned in
France, from 1814 to
1824.*

fter Napoleon returned to France from his Egyptian campaign in October 1799, he quickly executed a coup d'état, establishing himself as first consul. He announced that the revolution was over and declared that France would now consolidate its revolutionary gains. The new regime appeared to offer stability and peace to the French people after 10 years of turbulence, and they gave Napoleon wide support.

This development seriously affected the plans of Louis Stanislas Xavier (1755–1824), younger brother of the executed Louis XVI. Before the revolution, Stanislas had intrigued against his brother, and might have taken the king's place as constitutional monarch after 1789. But he sensed the dangerous way revolutionary winds were blowing and became an émigré, while his brother remained in France and was executed. Louis XVII, Stanilas's nephew, second son of Louis XVI, and next in the Bourbon line of succession,

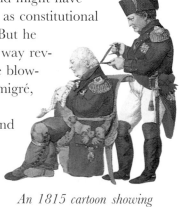

*An 1815 cartoon showing
Louis haunted by a ghost
returning from the empire.*

died in prison in 1795, only 10 years old. Until Napoleon took control, the coming to power of Louis XVIII (he assumed the title in 1795) seemed likely, for the people of France were exhausted by years of revolution and upheaval.

Louis had watched the rise of the young General Bonaparte with interest. In 1797, believing his restoration imminent, he offered Napoleon the viceroyalty of Corsica and the title of marshal of France if Napoleon would declare for him. However, a military coup in 1797 ousted the 53 royalist deputies Louis was hoping to use as his power base. Then came Bonaparte's famous coup (November 9, 1799). In some alarm Louis wrote

---

Biography

*N*apoleon Bonaparte (1769–1821), born in Corsica and educated in French military academies, made his name at the siege of Toulon in 1793, and proved an outstanding soldier when he commanded the French army in Italy (1796). Victories over the Austrians and a campaign in Egypt followed. Successful on land, Napoleon was checked at sea by Britain's Horatio Nelson in the Battle of the Nile (1798). In 1799 a coup d'état made him first consul of France, and he became emperor five years later. He eventually overextended himself militarily. Louis XVIII took the throne in 1814 and Napoleon was exiled. He escaped and attempted a return to power in 1815 but was defeated at Waterloo.

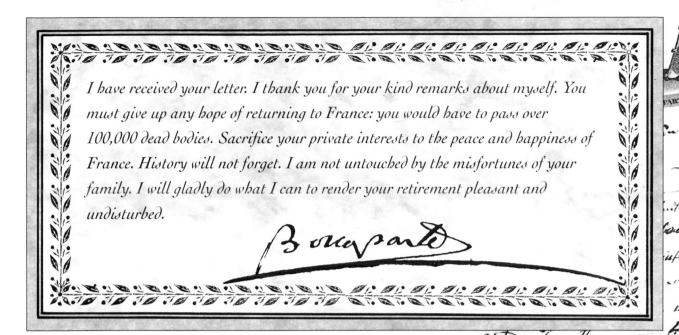

> *I have received your letter. I thank you for your kind remarks about myself. You must give up any hope of returning to France: you would have to pass over 100,000 dead bodies. Sacrifice your private interests to the peace and happiness of France. History will not forget. I am not untouched by the misfortunes of your family. I will gladly do what I can to render your retirement pleasant and undisturbed.*
>
> *Bonaparte*

to Napoleon in early 1800: "You are taking a long time to give me back my throne; there is a danger that you may miss the opportunity. Without me you cannot make France happy, while without you I can do nothing for France. So be quick and let me know what positions and dignities will satisfy you and your friends." Napoleon's prompt reply was devastatingly brief, and three years later, in 1803, he suggested to Louis that he face facts and give up his claims to the throne of France. The stubborn Bourbon refused. In 1804 Napoleon declared himself emperor.

Until 1814 the French received from their Corsican emperor everything they could have hoped for from a Bourbon restoration: an agreement with the church, a civil code, the rule of law, good roads, effective schools, and more. But Louis's hour came at last in 1814 when Napoleon was forced to abdicate after the Parisian authorities surrendered to the allied forces of Austria, Russia, Prussia, and Britain. Napoleon was granted the island of Elba, and went into exile.

King at last, Louis XVIII tried to turn the clock back to 1789, making the restoration unpopular. As a result, Napoleon was able to return from Elba in March 1815 and conduct the Hundred Days campaign, only to suffer final

Above: Napoleon crowning his empress, Josephine. As did the great emperor Charlemagne (742–814), Napoleon had the pope, who traveled to Paris for the occasion, officiate at his coronation. Like Charlemagne, Napoleon also took the crown from the pope and placed it on his own head, to show that he did not owe his earthly authority to the church.

defeat at Waterloo. When Napoleon surrendered and was sent into permanent exile on St. Helena, "Unite and forget" became Louis's motto. He would always admire Napoleon's military talent, and the novelist Honoré de Balzac would suggest that the two men in fact had much in common: "After every revolution, genius in government consists in effecting a fusion, which is what Napoleon and Louis XVIII did, both being men of true genius."

ROBERT E. LEE
TO
THE ARMY OF NORTHERN VIRGINIA

April 10, 1865

*The defeated Confederate general,
having surrendered to General Grant,
writes a formal letter of farewell to his army.*

*The portrait of Robert E. Lee
that hangs at Washington and
Lee University.*

Early in April of 1865, Robert E. Lee, the hero of the Confederacy, led the remnants of his battered Army of Northern Virginia out of Richmond (capital of the Southern Confederacy) on a do-or-die forced march, hoping ultimately to link up with Gen. Joseph E. Johnston's beleaguered army in the mountains of Virginia and Tennessee. But Gen. Ulysses S. Grant, the Union commander, pursued him relentlessly for a devastating week. After a military debacle on April 6—the "Black Thursday" of the Confederacy—Lee was reduced to 12,500 effectives, a third of the force with which he had retreated from Richmond. Seeing his enemy's plight, Grant called upon Lee on April 7 to surrender and avoid further bloodshed. Lee replied that he did not yet consider his position hopeless, but as he too wished to avoid unnecessary loss of life he asked what surrender terms Grant was prepared to offer, and requested a meeting at 10 A.M. on the 9th.

On the morning of April 9, General Lee rode to the Union lines under a flag of truce, escorted by just two men. Grant, 43 years old, was the victor over a distinguished commander 15 years his senior. He called for Lee's men to be disarmed, paroled, and disqualified from taking up arms again. By 4 P.M. all the copies of the surrender had been made and signed, and Grant had agreed to send 25,000 packs of rations to the starving Confederate army.

The following day Lee wrote his formal letter

ANG OUT YOUR BANNERS

UNION

VICTO

PEAC

Surrender of
eral Lee and
Whole Arr

THE WORK OF PAL

Final Triumph of th
the Potomac

The Strategy and Diplomacy of Lieut.-Gen.
Grant.

Terms and Conditions of the

Biography

Robert Edward Lee (1807–70) graduated second at West Point Military Academy in 1829 and served as chief engineer of the central army in the Mexican–American war (1846–48). He was severely wounded at Chapultepec in Mexico. After commanding the U.S. military academy and seeing service with the cavalry in Texas, Lee resigned his commission in 1861 to fight for the Confederacy. He became the highly successful commander of the Army of Northern Virginia. In February 1865 he was appointed general-in-chief of Confederate forces. After the war he became president of Washington College (now Washington and Lee University) at Lexington, Virginia.

*Above: the Southern
anthem, "God Save
the South"—a cover
illustration for the
sheet music.*

GOD SAVE THE SOUTH

Headquarters, Army of Northern Virginia,
April 10, 1865

After four years of arduous service, marked by unsurpassed courage and fortitude, the Army of Northern Virginia has been compelled to yield to overwhelming numbers and resources. I need not tell the survivors of so many hard-fought battles, who have remained steadfast to the last, that I have consented to this result from no distrust of them; but, feeling that valor and devotion could accomplish nothing that could compensate for the loss that would have attended the continuation of the contest, I have determined to avoid the useless sacrifice of those whose past services have endeared them to their countrymen. By the terms of the agreement, officers and men can return to their homes and remain there until exchanged. You will take with you the satisfaction that proceeds from the consciousness of duty faithfully performed; and I earnestly pray that a merciful God will extend to you His blessing and protection. With an increasing admiration of your constancy and devotion to your country, and a grateful remembrance of your kind and generous consideration of myself, I bid you an affectionate farewell.

R. E. Lee

Right: Weeping veterans of Lee's Army of Northern Virginia furl their flag for the last time in this painting by Richard Norris Brooke.

Below: A percussion-cap rifle of the 1860's

of farewell to his army. The one element of their defeat that Lee did not—perhaps could not—mention was that in his final campaign he had been consistently outmaneuvered. As one staff colonel said of Grant: "He commanded Lee's army as much as he did ours; caused and knew beforehand every movement that Lee made, up to the actual surrender . . . . There was no letup; fighting and marching, and negotiating, all at once."

KARL MARX
— TO —
FRIEDRICH ENGELS

November 30, 1867

*The socialist philosopher writes to
his friend and colleague expounding his ideas
on the future of Ireland.*

*Karl Marx
believed class-
consciousness
would overcome
animosity
between
Catholic and
Protestant.*

*Friedrich
Engels, himself
married to an
ardent Fenian,
had an Irish-
nationalist
outlook.*

The most dramatic development in Irish history in the 1860's was the growth of the Irish Republican Brotherhood, a secret, oath-bound organization better known as the Fenians. Founded in New York in 1858, and dedicated to the end of British rule, the Fenians quickly won thousands of supporters in Ireland (which had been ruled from London for over 250 years). In the United States a quarter of a million dollars was raised to finance an uprising in Ireland. There was a raid into Canada in 1866, and in January 1867 Fenian "wolves" (mostly Union veterans of the Civil War) set sail for Ireland to proclaim an Irish republic. The uprising was a failure.

Tensions crossed the sea to the British mainland. Liberal opinion in England knew that the Irish problem needed to be addressed. William Ewart Gladstone, who became prime minister in 1868 after a sweeping electoral victory, brought in a bill to disestablish the Protestant Church of Ireland. He had plans to legislate to protect the rights of tenants on the land, who were at the mercy of absentee landlords, and hoped to counteract a growing movement demanding Irish independence.

This was the context in which the father of "scientific socialism" Karl Marx wrote the words in the extract opposite from a letter to his great friend and collaborator Friedrich Engels (1820–95). Engels was a rich, retired businessman who

*Evictions of Irish tenant
farmers, such as this one by
a policeman supported by
troops, were frequent in poor
harvest years in the 1800's.*

Biography

Karl Marx (1818–83), founding father of modern communism, was born in Germany, the son of a Jewish lawyer. His collaboration with Friedrich Engels began in 1844. They jointly prepared the Communist Manifesto in 1847–48. Marx was forced to seek refuge in England after the convulsive revolutions of 1848, supported financially by Engels. In the 1860's he began his masterpiece, *Das Kapital*, a profound analysis of contemporary capitalism, still unfinished when he died. Engels completed the last two volumes from Marx's notes. Marx's later influence on world history was immense, and his grave in Highgate cemetery, London, became a place of pilgrimage for socialists.

If you have read the journals you will have seen that 1) the Memorial of the International Council for the Fenians was sent to Hardy, and that 2) the debate on Fenianism was public (last Tuesday week) and reported in The Times. I came very late (I ran a temperature for about a fortnight and the fever passed only two days ago) and really did not intend to speak, firstly because of my troublesome physical condition, and secondly because of the ticklish situation. Nevertheless Weston, who was in the chair, tried to force me to, so I moved that the meeting be adjourned. This obliged me to speak last Tuesday. As a matter of fact I had prepared for Tuesday last not a speech but the points of a speech. But the Irish reporters failed to come.

What the English do not yet know is that since 1846 the economic content and therefore also the political aim of English domination in Ireland have entered into an entirely new phase, and that, precisely because of this, the characteristic features of Fenianism are socialistic tendencies and the fact that it is a movement of the lower orders. What can be more ridiculous than to confuse the barbarities of Elizabeth or Cromwell, who wanted to supplant the Irish by English colonists, with the present system, which wants to supplant them by sheep, pigs and oxen! The stupid English Government in London knows nothing of course of this immense change since 1846. But the Irish know it. From Meagher's Proclamation (1848) down to the election manifesto of Hennesy (Tory and Urquhartite) (1866), the Irish have expressed their awareness of this in the clearest and most forcible manner.

The question now is, what advice shall we give to the English workers? What the Irish need is:

1) Self-government and independence from England.

2) An agrarian revolution. With the best intentions in the world the English cannot accomplish this for them, but they can give them the legal means of accomplishing it for themselves.

3) Protective tariffs against England. Between 1783 and 1801 all branches of Irish industry flourished. The Union, by abolishing the protective tariffs established by the Irish Parliament, destroyed all industrial life in Ireland. Once the Irish are independent, necessity will turn them into protectionists, as it did Canada, Australia, etc. Before I present my views in the Central Council (next Tuesday, this time fortunately without reporters), I should be glad if you gave me your opinion in a few lines.

Greetings

*Top: Homage on
Saint Patrick's Day 1874 in New York
to a nationalist with constitutional methods—a bust of
the conservative Catholic parliamentarian, Daniel O'Connell.*

*Above: A first lieutenant's certificate of rank in the
Provisional Army of the Fenian Brotherhood (1867).*

rode to hounds, was a member of gentlemen's clubs, and a patron of the Halle Orchestra. Always immaculately dressed, methodical and clearheaded, he contrasted strongly with the man whose life and work he so heavily subsidized. Marx was a man without a private income, who took no pride in his appearance, and whose study was a chaos of books and papers. Engels was self-taught, picked up his views from wide reading, and had experience in business and the military. Marx had a university background, and was strongly influenced by the German philosopher Hegel. In 1843, in Paris, he finally embraced communism. Engels concentrated his writing on military history, science, and the popularization of Marxism. Marx focused on political economy and the materialist theory of history.

To some extent these differences were reflected in the friends' respective views of

Ireland. Engels' heart ruled in his attitude to Ireland. His first great love was his mistress Mary Burns, an Irish working-class girl he met on his first visit to Manchester. With her, Engels toured Ireland in May 1856, and was left with a deep love of the country and a burning detestation of the history of British wrongdoing there.

With Marx, the head predominated in his attitude to Ireland. Unlike Engels, who saw the Fenians as the latest in a long line of Irish nationalists, Marx thought of Fenianism as a response to economic conditions in Ireland.

Marx regarded Fenianism as a species of socialism, believing that the interests of the English working class lay with an independent Ireland, and that the decisive blow to the English ruling class would be delivered in Ireland. His writings are full of the conviction that the English proletariat must detach itself from the Irish policies of the ruling class and make common cause with their Irish brothers. "The English working class *will never accomplish anything* until it has got rid of Ireland . . . . England never has and never can . . . rule Ireland otherwise than by the most abominable reign of terror and the most reprehensible corruption."

Divide-and-rule tactics

In Marx's view, Ireland was the bulwark of the English landed aristocracy. As matters stood, the English and Irish ruling class could use divide-and-rule tactics, setting English and Irish proletarians against each other, much as in the United States where the elite set blacks and "poor white trash" against each other.

Marx believed that it would be much easier to overthrow the aristocracy in Ireland, where the land question was a life-and-death issue, and where, in his view, the population was more passionate and revolutionary than the English. Ireland under the English yoke, said Marx, weakened the English proletariat by exporting cheap wool and meat, and by sending its surplus popu-

Above: Founding meeting of the International Workingmen's Association (later the First International), London, 1864. It aimed to unite workers divided by nationalism.

Right: Manifestos and pamphlets called on workers everywhere to unite.

lation to England, thus forcing down the people's wages.

As it turned out, Marx's predictions owed more to what he wanted than to sober analysis. When Gladstone disestablished the Irish Church, Marx thought this would also lead to the downfall of the Church of England, as well as the end of landlordism in England and Ireland. Once the Irish Church was dead, Protestant Irish tenants in Ulster would join the Catholics in the South, preventing landlords from exploiting religious antagonism. In the end, the nationalism in Ireland triumphed over class-consciousness, and the religious differences still continue, as bitter as ever.

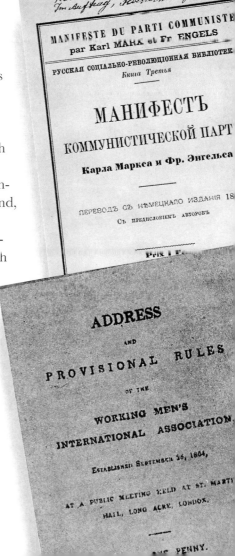

ÉMILE ZOLA
TO
THE PRESIDENT OF FRANCE

January 13, 1898

*In an open letter to the president of France,
the novelist Émile Zola accuses the Ministry of War
of a cover-up in the Dreyfus affair.*

*Émile Zola, as
he appeared in
the British
literary and
satirical review,
Vanity Fair,
in 1880.*

*Félix Faure,
president of France
from 1895 to
1899, who was a
militarist and a
declared anti-
Dreyfusard.*

For 12 years at the turn of the last century, France was split by an infamous miscarriage of justice. Even within families, loyalties were divided. The cause of all this was the Dreyfus affair. Such were the moral stakes that one of France's preeminent writers, Émile Zola, threw his name into the controversy at great personal cost and risk.

Capt. Alfred Dreyfus (1859–1935) was a French army officer with duties in the Ministry of War. He had an unblemished record, but when he was accused of selling military secrets to the Germans, two facts about his background helped to make him a target of suspicion: he was from Alsace—a territory once French but currently in German hands—and he was a Jew in an era of virulent antisemitism.

In 1894 a cleaning woman working for French Intelligence found evidence of spying in a wastebasket of the German military attaché in Paris. Colonel Henry, who was in charge of the investigations, pieced together fragments of a memo (called a *bordereau* in French). This listed five military documents the sender was giving to the German military attaché; the only clues were the initial D at the end and the handwriting.

Dreyfus was on the list of officers with access to the relevant information, and some

Biography

Born in Paris, the son of an Italian engineer, Émile Zola (1840–1902) began his career as a journalist and eventually achieved renown as a novelist. His best-known titles include *L'Assommoir* (1878), *Nana* (1880), *Germinal* (1885), and *La Bête Humaine* (1890). He was the leading exponent of "naturalism" in literature—the idea that a study of heredity and environment could provide an accurate picture of human personality. After the Dreyfus affair Zola faced continuing hostility from militaristic and antisemitic elements. He died in suspicious circumstances in his Paris apartment. At his funeral a crowd of more than 20,000 mourners followed his coffin while police held back hundreds who shouted abuse.

*Right: Onlookers
shouted "Jew!" and
"Traitor!" as Dreyfus's
buttons were ripped from his
uniform and his sword was
broken in two.*

Mr President,

Permit me, I beg you, in return for the gracious favor you once accorded me, to be concerned with regard to your just glory and to tell you that your record, so fair and fortunate thus far, is now threatened with the most shameful, the most ineffaceable blot.

What a clod of mud is flung upon your name—I was about to say your reign—through this abominable Dreyfus affair. A court martial has but recently, by order, dared to acquit one Esterhazy—a supreme slap at all truth, all justice! And it is done; France has this brand upon her visage; history will relate that it was during your administration that such a social crime could be committed.

I accuse Colonel du Paty de Clam of having been the diabolical agent of the judicial wrong, unconsciously, I prefer to believe, and of having continued to defend his deadly work during the past three years through the most absurd and revolting machinations.

I accuse General Mercier of having made himself an accomplice in one of the greatest crimes of the century, probably through weak-mindedness.

I accuse General Billot of having had in his hands decisive proofs of the innocence of Dreyfus and of having concealed them, and of having rendered himself guilty of the crime of lèse-humanité and lèse-justice, out of political motives and to save the face of the General Staff.

Finally, I accuse the first court-martial of having violated all human right in condemning a prisoner on testimony kept secret from him, and I accuse the second court-martial of having covered up this illegality by order, committing in its turn the judicial crime of knowingly acquitting a guilty man.

I have one passion only—light, in the name of humanity which has borne so much and has a right to happiness. My burning protest is only the cry of my soul. Let them dare, then, to carry me to the Court of Assizes, and let there be an inquiry in the full light of day!

I am waiting.

Mr President, I beg you to accept the assurances of my deepest respect.

Emile Zola

handwriting experts judged that his handwriting matched that on the *bordereau*. The minister of war, General Mercier, ordered his arrest, and his presumed guilt was widely reported in nationalistic newspapers. Court-martialed and found guilty, Dreyfus continued to protest his innocence, but the country was in no mood to listen. People wanted a proof of treachery—to confirm a view that only betrayal had made it possible for Germany to humiliate France in the Franco-Prussian War more than 20 years earlier. After a public degradation in which he was stripped of his rank, Dreyfus was transported to Devil's Island, to a living death in a French penal colony off the French Guiana coast.

The true spy discovered

More than a year later came a dramatic twist. Aware of the weakness of their case, the military chiefs had instructed Col. Georges Picquart to find more evidence against Dreyfus. Picquart discovered that the incriminating wastebasket had also contained fragments of a letter addressed to Maj. Charles Walsin Esterhazy, thanking him for information. Esterhazy's handwriting exactly matched that on the *bordereau*.

Picquart informed his superiors. "What difference does it make to you if that Jew remains on Devil's Island?" they asked. Picquart was then sent on a mission far from the Ministry of War.

Below: "I accuse . . . !"—the issue of L'Aurore *which gave over its front page to Zola's open letter accusing high-ranking officers in the Dreyfus affair.*

Dreyfus's brother Mathieu, meanwhile, had also stumbled onto Esterhazy's trail and publicly accused him of the crime for which his brother was paying the penalty. There followed so great a groundswell of pro-Dreyfus feeling, particularly among the intelligentsia, that a court-martial of Esterhazy became unavoidable. The military closed ranks and acquitted him.

This was the situation when, on January 13, 1898, Émile Zola wrote his open letter to Félix Faure, excerpted here. As Zola had intended, he was tried for libel, and at the trial all the army's corruption and double-dealing in the Dreyfus affair was revealed. Nevertheless, Zola was found guilty and fined 3,000 francs plus 12 months in jail. Recognizing that he would lose an appeal, he fled to England.

The price of speaking out

When he wrote the open letter, Zola was one of the richest and most famous novelists in France, at the peak of his success. The letter, and his novel *La Débâcle* (1892), with its portrayal of the army's incompetence in the Franco-Prussian War, had made him a marked man. Exile in England was the heavy price he paid: he did not speak English, disliked the food and the climate, missed his family and friends, and was unable to work.

Yet his trial and conviction had an impact, helping to focus the public's attention upon the Dreyfus affair. France thereafter was divided rigidly into two opposing camps. In a last-ditch attempt at damage limitation, the army dismissed the honest Picquart; but on August 30, 1898, Colonel Henry confessed his forgeries and slit his own throat. Esterhazy fled to England, where he too admitted his guilt. Finally, in June 1899 the verdict on Dreyfus was set aside and a new trial was ordered. Zola came home from England, and Dreyfus from Devil's Island. By this time Dreyfus was seriously ill and prematurely aged,

but sustained by the thought that he would be vindicated. Incredibly, the second court-martial, on September 9, 1899, found him guilty but with "extenuating circumstances," and sentenced him to 10 years' imprisonment. President Faure pardoned him 10 days later on grounds of ill-health, but as Zola said: "Even Jesus was condemned but once." Dreyfus continued to seek justice, and on July 12, 1906, he was proclaimed innocent at last. Reinstated in the army with full honors, he was promoted to major and was made a member of the Légion d'Honneur.

Above: Military dash turns heads in the Paris of the 1890's (a painting by Jean Béraud).

Below: Cards sent to Dreyfus by sympathizers while he was on Devil's Island.

NEVILLE CHAMBERLAIN
TO
ADOLF HITLER

September 23, 1938

*The British prime minister sums up
his discussions with the German fuehrer
during the Sudetenland crisis.*

*Neville
Chamberlain, who
told the British
people that the
Munich agreement
meant "peace for
our time."*

*Adolf Hitler, who
followed his
assurances at Munich
with invasions and
military occupations
that put most of
Europe in his grasp.*

In 1938, the 3 million German-speaking inhabitants of the Sudeten region of Czechoslovakia agitated for a union with Germany, and the German fuehrer, Adolf Hitler, was more than willing to have them. Britain assumed the role of mediator in the diplomatic conflict which now blew up.

Neville Chamberlain, the British prime minister, was determined to prevent a major war and hoped that by appeasing Hitler, he could keep Germany from escalating its demands and igniting international tensions. First Chamberlain detached France—which had a mutual defense treaty with Czechoslovakia—

from its ally, convincing the French that they could not defend Czechoslovakia anyway. Then he sent his envoy, Lord Runciman, to mediate in talks between the Czech president Eduard Benes and the Sudeten Germans, pressing Benes to agree to demands for more Sudeten autonomy.

When a faction of Sudeten Germans revolted in favor of union with Germany on September 13, Benes's government put the rebellion down by force. Fearing Germany would invade Czechoslovakia, Chamberlain offered Hitler the Sudetenland. The French grew alarmed, and their premier, Edouard Daladier, went to London to argue that Hitler's true aim was the domination of Europe. Chamberlain agreed to guarantee the independence of the truncated Czechoslovakia that was envisaged, and Benes was forced to accept the deal under threat that otherwise he would lose the support of Britain and France. Chamberlain went to Germany twice in September for meetings to help set the seal on the agreement. Hitler wanted immediate German occupation of the Sudetenland, and it is this demand that Chamberlain addresses in the shortened version of his letter to the German

Biography

Neville Chamberlain (1869–1940) was the son of the celebrated British politician Joseph Chamberlain and brother to Austen Chamberlain (British foreign secretary and Nobel Prize winner). A skillful administrator, he was mayor of Birmingham, chancellor of the exchequer, and minister for health before becoming prime minister of a coalition government in 1937. His policy of appeasement toward Hitler and Mussolini reflected the mood of Britain in the 1930's, but it played into the hands of the dictators. He was forced to resign in favor of a more belligerent Winston Churchill in 1940.

I think it may clarify the situation and accelerate our conversation if I send you this note before we meet this morning.

The difficulty I see about the proposal you put to me yesterday afternoon arises from the suggestion that the areas should in the immediate future be occupied by German troops. I am sure that an attempt to occupy forthwith by German troops areas which will become part of the Reich at once in principle, and very shortly afterwards by formal delimitation, would be condemned as an unnecessary display of force. The immediate question before us is how to maintain law and order pending the final settlement of the arrangements for the transfer. I could ask the Czech Government whether they think there could be an arrangement under which the maintenance of law and order in certain agreed Sudeten German areas would be entrusted to the Sudeten Germans themselves. The Czech Government cannot, of course, withdraw their forces, so long as they are faced with the prospect of forcible invasion; but I would urge them to withdraw from the areas where the Sudeten Germans are in a position to maintain order.

I am,
Yours faithfully,

N Chamberlain

Above: An irreverent darts game of the late 1930's features the leading political figures involved in the crisis.

Left: Sudetenlanders saluting German occupation forces on their arrival in the disputed territory on October 1, 1938.

fuehrer that appears here. In Munich on September 29, a conference between Britain, France, Germany, and Italy—the Czechs were excluded—gave Hitler all he wanted. But in March 1939 Germany annexed what was left of Czechoslovakia. When Hitler invaded Poland in September 1939, it was clear that the policy of appeasement had failed hopelessly, and a reluctant Chamberlain declared war on Germany.

John Maynard Keynes
to
Kingsley Wood

October 16, 1943

*Britain's foremost economist reports to his government
on the negotiations that led to the establishment of the
International Monetary Fund and the World Bank.*

*John Maynard
Keynes, 1st
Baron of
Tilton, who
advocated the
use of economic
policy to achieve
social goals.*

*Howard
Kingsley Wood,
who was the
British
chancellor of
the exchequer
(finance
minister).*

From 1941 to 1943 the brilliant British economist John Maynard Keynes was almost continually involved in negotiations with the United States on the world economic order that would emerge once the Axis powers were defeated. The problem: to create a new world order with monetary stability, in which conflicting national economic interests could be reconciled.

Keynes and Harry Dexter White, the chief assistant to the U.S. treasury secretary, put forward rival plans to stabilize currencies by offering protection against short-term balance-of-payments crises. Keynes wanted for Britain a postwar regime of full employment, low interest rates, and high prices; in other words, he wanted international cooperation and domestic inflation. White, on the other hand, wanted it to be a condition of any International Monetary Fund that the member nations should refrain from inflating.

The eventual compromise was later accepted by a world economic conference at Bretton Woods, New Hampshire, in July 1944. In his letter to Kingsley Wood (the British chancellor of the exchequer), an abstract of which appears on the right, Keynes expresses his satisfaction that an agreement has proved possible.

The International Monetary Fund was then established with

Above: Initial unease in the British press. "Is this the only way?" asks a borrowing John Bull in 1945 as he heads into the woods.

initial deposits of $8.8 billion (Keynes had wanted $25 billion and White $8 billion). National access to the fund was not to be automatic, as in the original Keynes plan, but neither could the fund demand changes in domestic economic policy, as

---

Biography

John Maynard Keynes (1883–1946), perhaps the greatest economist of the century, came from an academic family and was a fellow of King's College, Cambridge. Chief economic adviser to the Treasury at the Versailles Peace Conference, he strenuously opposed the peace terms and resigned in protest. He followed his brilliant *Treatise on Probability* with *A Treatise on Money* and the revolutionary and original *General Theory of Employment, Interest and Money* (1936). Keynes's insistence on full employment as the prime goal of economic policy deeply influenced President F.D. Roosevelt. Keynes played a leading part in planning the postwar financial structure of the world.

All the relevant American departments were present and were satisfied with the result, in particular the State Department and the Federal Reserve Board. We are all of us agreed that the atmosphere could not have been better and that the progress is far in excess of our best expectations. The American Departments, and particularly the State Department, were exceedingly coy and slow in accepting the necessity of primary Anglo-American cooperation. But after a little experience of it they have embraced it with both hands. There is no risk, I should say, of the old standoffish attitude. All the committees have worked together constructively and fruitfully, and it is most unlikely that the civil servants, whatever the politicians may feel, will want to return either to isolationism on the one hand, or to the method of the grand monkey house on the other. The Americans started with a totally different point of view from ours. They thought of the Fund as an active, benevolent institution which would study the advisability of every transaction and O.K. it or not as a faithful schoolmistress. What they had in view would clearly cut right across international banking arrangements as they have existed hitherto. It was a very great concession on their part to come round to our view of the Fund as a reserve resource, entirely passive, except in the more extreme contingencies where countries were running towards the limit of the facilities of the Fund in one direction or another.

Keynes

Right: Surplus Brazilian coffee dumped in the sea in 1932. The Bretton Woods agreement aimed to avoid the economic chaos of the 1930's.

in the original White plan. The key currency was to be the dollar, fixed at a price of $35 a gold ounce, and the only currency redeemable in gold. This involved moving the financial center of the world from London to Washington.

The new system worked well until the early 1970's, when U.S. payments deficits meant that the dollar could no longer function as the anchoring currency. Only then were fixed exchange rates abandoned.

WINSTON CHURCHILL
— TO —
LORD QUICKSWOOD

July, 1945

*Britain's wartime leader
expresses his bewilderment at his
party's electoral defeat.*

*Winston Churchill, who was
not accepted as a peacetime
leader until 1951.*

Winston Churchill had presided over a World War II coalition for five years; he had stepped in to lead his country in the face of a threatened German invasion in 1940, and he had guided Britain to victory alongside her allies. In July 1945 he was midway through the Potsdam Conference, negotiating with Joseph V. Stalin of the Soviet Union and Harry S. Truman, the new U.S. president, when the news broke. It came as a profound shock to the prime minister to learn that he had just been turned out of office.

Immediately after the defeat of Germany on VE-Day, May 8, 1945, the Conservative and Labour parties in Britain agreed that an election should be held without waiting for the conclusion of the war with Japan. The last British poll had taken place 10 years earlier—men and women up to the age of 31 had never had the opportunity to vote.

The 1945 general election was unusual in that polling in Britain took place on Thursday, July 5, but counting did not take place until July 25, to allow all the votes cast by those serving in the military forces overseas to be registered. Not until July 26 was the announcement made. Churchill's letter refers to the sensational result. Labour won 393 seats out of 640, a majority of 146 over all other parties—and the greatest landslide since the Liberal victory of 1906. The Conservative Party was dramatically reduced to a mere 213 seats.

What caused this startling electoral reversal? One hypothesis suggests that the behavior of American servicemen stationed in Britain had served to alienate public opinion toward the U.S. The Conservative Party,

Below: Churchill memorabilia kept at his country residence, Chartwell House in Kent, spans a political career from 1900 to 1955.

Biography

Sir Winston Churchill (1874–1965) fought in the Sudan (1898), and was a war reporter in the Boer War (1899–1902). He became home secretary in 1910 and First Lord of the Admiralty in 1911, resigning after a disastrous defeat at Gallipoli in 1915. He was called in as prime minister in 1940 when German invasion seemed imminent. There followed his "finest hour" as a war-time leader of exceptional courage and vision. Though he was defeated in the 1945 election, he returned as prime minister in 1951. In 1953 he won the Nobel Prize for Literature and was made an honorary U.S. citizen in 1963.

Chequers, 29 July 1945

My dear Linky

I must confess I found the event of Thursday rather odd and queer, especially after the wonderful welcomes I had from all classes. There was something pent-up in the British people after twenty years which required relief. It is like 1906 over again.

My faith in the flexibility of our Constitution and in the qualities of the British people remains unaltered. We must expect great changes which will be hard for the departing generation to adapt themselves to. The next two years will present administrative difficulties of an unprecedented character, and it may well be that a Labour administration will have a much better chance of solving these than we. I agree with you that their internal stresses will soon become acute.

Winston S. Churchill

particularly associated with Britain's "special relationship" with the U.S. was caught in the prevailing mood of anti-Americanism. The public viewed the Labour Party, on the other hand, as more closely aligned with "our heroic allies, the Russians"—wartime friends who were all the more popular and heroic as the British people had seen nothing of them. Perhaps more meaningful in the Conservatives' fall from power was the widespread peacetime unemployment the 1930's had seen under their leadership. Nobody wanted a return to the bad old days. While people regarded Churchill as a great wartime leader, they regarded him as unreliable in peacetime, pointing with misgivings to his dubious record in troubled Ireland and India, and to his handling

of Britain's General Strike of 1926. Most importantly, hordes of servicemen returned from the world war prepared to challenge the old class-ridden way of life the Conservatives seemed to represent. The Labour Party appeared to offer the British people a chance for a different future.

Churchill would live another 20 years, long enough to be recalled to leadership and to be honored internationally.

Right: A campaign-weary Churchill and his daughter Sarah picnic by the roadside during an electioneering tour of Britain in June 1945.

Below: The Evening Standard *for July 26, 1945, broadcasts the news: with 101 seats still to be declared, the Conservative Party had conceded an overwhelming Labour victory.*

YURI ANDROPOV
TO
SAMANTHA SMITH

1982

*The Soviet president tells
an American schoolgirl that his country
is devoted to peace.*

Yuri Andropov, whose brief period as ruler of the Soviet Union prepared the way for later attempts at reform.

Samantha Smith, whose honest letter of appeal won the hearts of people on both sides of the Cold War.

The early 1980's was a period of acute tension between the superpowers, perhaps the worst since the 1962 Cuban missile crisis. NATO deployed U.S. cruise missiles in Europe, the Soviets invaded Afghanistan, and the arms race was in full swing. Such was the context in 1982 when a 10-year-old American schoolgirl, Samantha Smith, wrote from her home in Manchester, Maine, to Soviet leader Yuri Andropov. In her letter Samantha expressed her anxiety that the U.S. and the U.S.S.R. would fight a nuclear war. With touching artlessness, Samantha asked Andropov: "Why do you want to conquer the whole world, or at least our country?"

Andropov responded to Samantha with the diplomatic letter abbreviated here, in which he claimed that his country's intentions were peaceful. Samantha's subsequent visit to the Soviet Union was a great personal triumph for her. She met top Kremlin officials, had lunch with the first woman cosmonaut, and saw the Kirov Ballet in Leningrad (St. Petersburg). Samantha was a natural ambassador.

The visit was also a triumph for Andropov and his country, for it brought the letter and Andropov's skillful response into public view, and in the process generated a wave of goodwill toward the Soviet Union. When Samantha appeared on prime-time talk shows in the U.S., her honesty and simplicity bridged the antagonisms between her country and the one she had visited. In retrospect, there is something poignant about this exchange. Andropov,

Above: A "perestroika" badge. This reform movement owed much to Andropov.

Biography

Yuri Andropov (1914–84), Soviet public official, was born in the northern Caucasus, the son of a railwayman. He became a youth organizer and then (1939–51) a Communist Party official in Karelia. Entering the foreign ministry in 1953, he was Soviet ambassador to Hungary at the time of the 1956 uprising, and in 1967 was appointed head of the KGB. In 15 years he professionalized the service, controlled its worst excesses, and made it more respectable. In 1973 he was appointed to the Politburo. On the death of Leonid Brezhnev in 1982 he became general secretary of the Communist Party, and in 1983 head of the Soviet Presidium.

аманта!

вое письмо
й страны, и

ется, — я с
кая на Бэкки
ественника
все мальчи

ешь, что о
нашими стр
вспыхнут

опрос — са
ловек. От

аманта, м
ло войны
ак хочет к
нашего го

етские люд
нацистска
м, напала
одов и сел

ой войне,
ными Шта
ков многих
по И сег
всеми сво
конечно

у Америк
жет в один
ибо было
на весь м
е первым н
го дальней
ов на Земл

★

Dear Samantha,

I received your letter, which is like many others that have reached me from your country and from other countries around the world. It seems to me that you are a courageous and honest girl, resembling Becky, the friend of Tom Sawyer in the famous book of your compatriot Mark Twain.

Soviet people well know what a terrible thing war is. Forty-two years ago, Nazi Germany attacked our country, burned and destroyed many thousands of our towns and villages, killed millions of Soviet men, women and children. In that war we were in an alliance with the United States. And today we want very much to live in peace, to trade and cooperate with all our neighbors on this earth. And certainly with such a great country as the United States of America.

In America and in our country there are nuclear weapons — terrible weapons that can kill millions of people in an instant. But we do not want them ever to be used. That's precisely why the Soviet Union solemnly declared throughout the entire world that never — never — will it use nuclear weapons first against any country.

I invite you, if your parents will let you, to come to our country, the best time being the summer. See for yourself: in the Soviet Union everyone is for peace and for friendship among peoples.

Thank you for your letter. I wish you all the best in your young life.

Andropov

who introduced some reform in the Soviet Union, died of kidney failure in 1984. A year later Samantha at 13, was killed in a plane crash on a domestic flight. President Ronald Reagan waived diplomatic protocol so that the Soviet Embassy could be represented at the funeral. Samantha's mother set up the Samantha Smith Center devoted to exchange visits for Soviet and American children. A decade after this exchange of letters, the threat of nuclear war had all but disappeared; in fact, the Soviet Union no longer existed.

Top: A Pioneer badge symbolizing all Soviet children.

Above: Samantha at a Pioneer camp.

LOVE, DEATH
&
FRIENDSHIP

*O*utpourings of love, grief, and despair; messages of support and reassurance; expressions of anxiety and irritation—most of us have bundles of such letters kept locked away, to be perused many years later, when the passions have faded and even the memories have grown dim. Apart from straightforward business communications, letters of love and friendship, and letters surrounding the moment of death, are perhaps the most common kind of missive; they bring our thoughts and emotions to the attention of another—the object of, or sympathizers with, our feelings. These, more than any others, are the letters that attract the curiosity of later readers. Deeply felt words, set down in the heat of the moment, have their own kind of truth. They are also the most direct, usually written in the hand of the sender. Even the paper they are written on may display signs of true emotion—a tearstain, a dab of perfume, a drop of blood. When famous men and women write such letters, they tend to be bound up with the great events of history. Horatio Nelson, the English naval hero, wrote unguarded, even salacious, letters to his mistress Emma Hamilton, and the note he jotted down to her on the eve of the fateful Battle of Trafalgar intrigues us both for its snapshot of an admiral's feelings before a battle, and for its insight into a notorious love affair. The Roman writer Cicero managed to make an elegant joke to his friend and ally Atticus out of a description of an awkward visit from his powerful political enemy, Julius Caesar. Others were more outspoken in criticism and in the process touched on fundamental issues facing their age. When D. H. Lawrence complained in intemperate language of the philosopher Bertrand Russell's intellectuality and political traditionalism, he highlighted some of the deepest dilemmas of the 20th century; and the protest from Carl Jung that his mentor Sigmund Freud treated his pupils as children expressed its author's mixed feelings of anger, love, frustration, and dedication, while identifying problems at the heart of psychoanalysis.

Letters surrounding death are often more self-conscious. The explorer Captain Scott, aware of the power of the dying hero, spent his last hours in an Antarctic blizzard drafting letters to his family, friends, sponsors, and the wives of his companions, composing the account of his exploits that would become legendary. For men and women sentenced to execution, the last letter became part of their final statement to the world: many a reputation has been salvaged by a brave performance on the scaffold. Thus the letter before the execution of John Brown consummated his lifelong campaign for the abolition of slavery, setting the seal on a career that would make his name a byword for the Union cause. And Abraham Lincoln's letter of condolence to a mother bereaved in pursuit of that cause is as eloquent as the Gettysburg Address in approaching the countless personal tragedies of Civil War America. Both of these men wrote with half an eye to posterity, and gave their words a universality that still transcends the struggles of their age.

CICERO
TO
ATTICUS

December, 45 B.C.

*The eminent Roman statesman describes
with some relief a successful evening spent
entertaining Julius Caesar.*

*Marcus Tullius Cicero, who
favored the old Roman republic
over personal despotism.*

On December 19, 45 B.C., two leading figures in the Roman world dined together in the town of Puteoli in southern Italy. Opposite is an abstract of the letter that Cicero, the host of this dinner, sent soon afterward to his childhood friend Titus Pomponius Atticus, a rich noble and successful businessman who acted as Cicero's literary adviser. Underlying Cicero's distinct relief at being finished with the disruption to his home and the great expense of entertaining his guest, there is a note of relief at regaining his distance from a dangerous man whose political ambitions he could not approve.

At the time of the visit, Marcus Tullius Cicero was a 61-year-old lawyer and statesman, the greatest orator and trial lawyer of his age. He belonged to an ancient

*Left: Romans of Cicero's time wrote
most of their correspondence on
papyrus from Egypt.*

and respectable family from Arpinum in central Italy, which before his time had never ventured beyond local politics. As a young man, Marcus Tullius had determined to change that, to become a "new man," as those who did not have "old money" to back them were known in Rome.

Cicero's excellent education and his brother Quintus's marriage to Atticus's sister helped him achieve his ambition. Cicero built on these beginnings to make a glittering career in law.

Cicero was eventually elected to all the great posts in Roman life, culminating in his appointment as consul (chief magistrate). As consul

---

Biography

Marcus Tullius Cicero (106–43 B.C.), born at Arpinum, made his name as a lawyer at 26 by successfully defending his client against a favorite of the dictator Sulla. He was then elected quaestor and praetor (magistrates of increasing importance) and in a great speech supported the appointment of Pompey to conduct a war against Mithridates of Pontus (Turkey). As consul he crushed the conspiracy of Catiline (63 B.C.). He remained neutral, for the most part, in the civil war between Caesar and Pompey, and retired from public life to write on rhetoric and philosophy. In 43 B.C., after Caesar's death, he delivered the famous speeches against Mark Antony that cost him his life.

Strange that so onerous a guest should leave a memory not disagreeable! It was really very pleasant. But when he arrived at Philippus' place on the evening of December 18, the house was so thronged by the soldiers that there was hardly a spare room for Caesar himself to dine in. Two thousand men, no less! I was a good deal perturbed about what would happen next day. On the 19th Caesar stayed with Philippus, he took a walk on the shore. Toward two he went to his bath. After anointing he took his place at dinner. He was following a course of emetics, and so both ate and drank with uninhibited enjoyment. It was really a fine, well-appointed meal. His entourage moreover were lavishly entertained in three other dining-rooms. The humbler freedmen and slaves had all they wanted—the smarter ones I entertained in style. In a word, I showed I knew how to live. But my guest was not the kind of person to whom one says, "Do come again when you are next in the neighborhood." Once is enough. We talked of nothing serious, but a good deal on literary matters. All in all, he was pleased and enjoyed himself. He said he would spend a day at Puteoli and another at Baiae.

There you are—a visit, or should I call it a billeting, which as I said was troublesome to me but not disagreeable.

CICERO

Above: Two contrasting messages in coin—a denarius bearing the head of Caesar (first Roman so honored in his own lifetime), and a later coin celebrating his assassination.

Cicero suppressed a major conspiracy against the state led by Catiline and received great acclaim. However, the execution of the conspirators without a proper trial eventually destroyed Cicero's reputation. For the next 15 years he was on the margins of Roman politics, though still in demand for the great legal cases.

Cicero's guest was Gaius Julius Caesar, famous as the greatest general of his age—a man whose immense political power could make a host nervous, especially one known for disagreeing with the principle of one-man rule. Caesar's star rose at about the same time as Cicero's, and by 60 B.C., he had become one of the three most powerful men in Rome. With the plutocrat Marcus Crassus and the general Gnaeus Pompeius Magnus (Pompey), Caesar had ruled Rome and its overseas empire.

However, this triumvirate did not last, and Caesar would not remain content with only a third share of the Roman empire. Caesar's share was Gaul (today France) and the countries to the north. For nearly

Right: A Roman inkwell and pen, for a letter-writer of the first century B.C.

10 years he engaged in fierce fighting, which ended in triumph for him: Gaul was subdued, Britain was invaded, and the German and Swiss tribes were driven back outside safe frontiers. However, Crassus was killed in 53 B.C. fighting the Parthians at Carrhae (Haran), in what is now southeast Turkey, and Pompey prepared for a trial of strength with Caesar. He and his supporters in the Senate ordered Caesar to disband his armies, but with the enthusiastic support of his legions Caesar defeated Pompey in a prolonged civil war. Caesar then forced the Senate to name him absolute ruler for a 10-year period. Cicero played only a small role in this conflict, supporting first Pompey and then Caesar.

Cicero and Caesar were very different men. Cicero believed in the virtues of the old Roman republic. Although longwinded, his prose was elegant and provides important historical records. Caesar—a ruthless, power-seeking politician and a great general—believed above all in his own star and wrote with economy and lucidity.

Yet Caesar remained always indulgent toward Cicero. He remembered that when the anti-Caesar faction had tried to pin responsibility for the Catiline conspiracy on him, Cicero refused to have anything to do with the accusation. Caesar regretted that Cicero seemed to dislike him personally, but Cicero denied disliking him. His quarrel with Caesar centered on the great man's desire to destroy the old Roman republic in favor of personal despotism.

Three months after the dinner took place, Caesar lay dead, slain by the assassins in the Senate on the Ides of March (March 15, 44 B.C). The suspicion arose that Cicero had been a ringleader of the conspirators. The rumor that Brutus, the most eminent of them, lifted aloft his dagger dripping with Caesar's blood and cried "Cicero!" seemed to lend considerable credence to this suspicion.

Although Cicero was in Rome on March 15, however, it seems unlikely that he knew of the assassination plot. Indeed, he had previously agreed with Caesar that the only conceivable result of the dictator's death would be another round of civil war. When Mark Antony and Octavian came forward to take up Caesar's mantle, Cicero denounced Mark Antony bitterly in a series of highly critical speeches, the *Philippics*. Mark Antony and two others (Lepidus and Octavian, later to be the emperor Augustus) had established a new triumvirate to rule Rome. They agreed to proscribe Cicero, and sought his execution and the confiscation of all his property. In 43 B.C., after many futile attempts to escape, Cicero was murdered as he rode in his litter.

In his *Second Philippic* Cicero provides his overall assessment of Caesar: "Caesar was a man of genius, intellect and memory, literate and careful, with the ability to plan and the industry to execute. His military achievements, though disastrous to the state, were immense.

"He planned a monarchy for many years and labored through immense dangers to effect his plan. By his gifts, public works, distributions of food and public hospitality, he reconciled the uneducated masses to his rule. He attached his supporters to him by rewards, his enemies by a show of mercy. In brief, partly by fear, partly by resignation to their lot, he imposed on a free republic the habit of subservience."

This page: Selections from a whimsical Roman floor mosaic of litter left by banqueters.

Opposite: Floor mosaic of a Roman banquet with music, first or second century A.D.

ABELARD
— TO —
HELOISE

1135

*The great thinker implores
Heloise to come to terms with
their fate and the will of God.*

*Heloise and Abelard, star-crossed lovers of the 12th
century, discoursing in a 15th-century manuscript.*

 eter Abelard was a highly original thinker and a brilliant teacher, debater, and theologian. In 1115 he became a lecturer in the cathedral school of Notre Dame in Paris. In the precincts of Notre Dame lived Heloise, niece of the canon, Fulbert. She was tall, fair, and striking at 17—though not especially beautiful—and already famous for her intellect and erudition. Her parents had died and left her penniless, but Fulbert had raised her himself and given her the best education possible. She wrote and spoke Latin, read Greek, and had an encyclopedic knowledge of the classics and the church fathers. Fulbert wanted contact with the very best minds for his niece; he hired Abelard as a tutor and welcomed him into his house. Abelard was 21 years older than Heloise, but they soon became lovers.

When Heloise became pregnant, Abelard took her away by night to his sister's home in Brittany, where she bore a son, Astralabe. When Abelard informed the enraged Canon Fulbert, the uncle agreed that the lovers must marry. This meant that Abelard could not become a priest and that his brilliant theological career would be ended—a revenge that gave Fulbert some satisfaction. Heloise, opposing the plan, quoted Saint Paul, Saint Jerome, and Cicero on the dubious benefits of marriage: "What concord is there between pupils and serving-maids, desks and cradles, books or tables and distaffs, pens

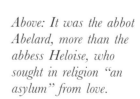

Above: It was the abbot Abelard, more than the abbess Heloise, who sought in religion "an asylum" from love.

Right: 13th-century seal of the University of Paris.

Biography

Peter Abelard (1079–1142), French theologian and philosopher, was born at Le Pallet, 10 miles southeast of Nantes, the eldest son of a noble Breton house. He sacrificed his inheritance to study philosophy, especially logic, and became a spellbinding lecturer on theology. His teaching on the Trinity was declared heretical in 1121 at the synod of Soissons. Despite recanting some of the doctrines that had given most offense, at the end of his life he was found guilty of heresy by the pope and the council of Sens. Beloved by his pupils, he aroused the hostility of the church's leaders by the originality of his work and his challenge to some of the traditional teachings of Christianity.

To the bride of Christ, Christ's servant.

The whole of your last letter is given up to a recital of your misery over the wrongs you suffer. First you complain that, contrary to custom in letter-writing, my letter to you put your name before mine in its greeting. Second, that when I ought to have offered you some remedy for your comfort I actually increased your sense of desolation. Third you went on to your old perpetual complaint against God concerning the manner of our entry into religious life and the cruelty of the act of treachery performed on me. Lastly, you set your self-accusations against my praise for you. . . . Say no more, I beg you, and cease from complaints like these which are far removed from the true depths of love! Yet even if you are still offended by this, I am so critically placed in daily despair of life that it is proper for me to take thought for the welfare of my soul and to provide for it while I may.

I come at last to your old perpetual complaint in which you presume to blame God for the manner of our entry into religion instead of wishing to glorify him as you justly should. I had thought that this bitterness of heart at what was so clear an act of divine mercy had long since disappeared. Recall what you have written, that in the manner of our conversion, when God seems to have been more my adversary, he has clearly shown himself kinder.

After our marriage, when you were living in the cloister at Argenteuil and I came to visit you privately, you know what my uncontrollable desire did with you there. . . . You know too how when you were pregnant and I took you to my own country you disguised yourself in the sacred habit of a nun, a pretense which was an irreverent mockery of the religion you now profess.

Come, my inseparable companion, and join me in thanksgiving. . . . Accept patiently what mercifully befell us. This is a father's rod not a persecutor's sword. The father strikes to correct, and to forestall the enemy who strikes to kill.

ABELARD

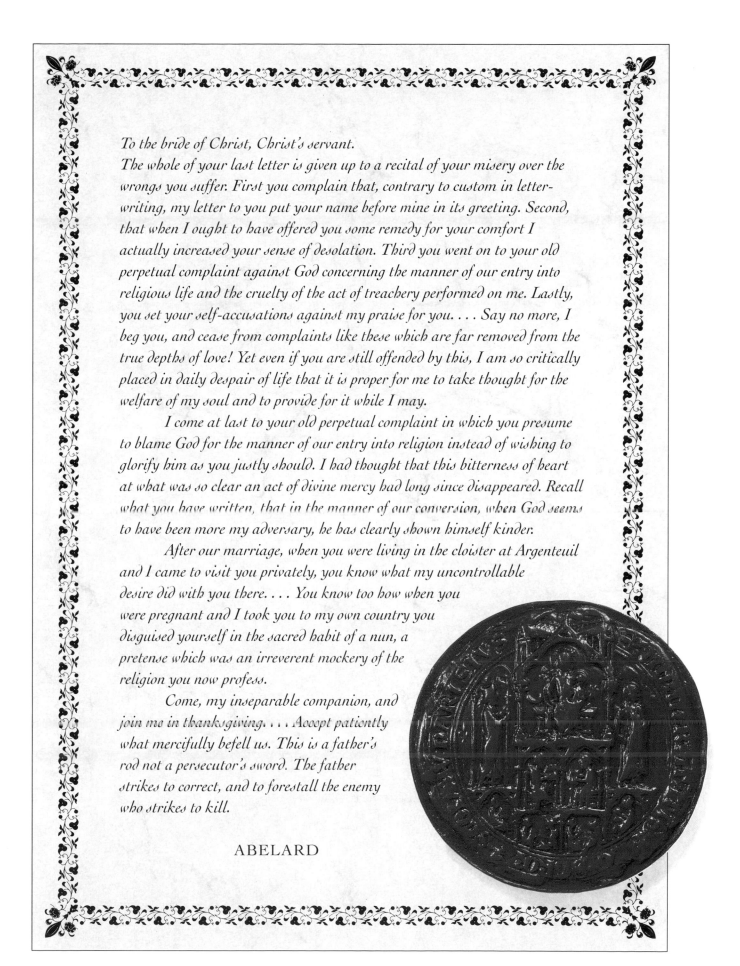

and spindles? Who, intent upon sacred or philosophic meditation, can endure the wailing of children, the lullabies of the nurses soothing them, the tumultuous mob of the household?" Eventually she agreed to the marriage only under extreme pressure from Abelard.

Leaving Astralabe with his aunt in Brittany, the couple returned to Paris and were married secretly in Fulbert's presence. At Heloise's insistence, they separated immediately afterward. She still hoped that if the marriage was kept secret, her lover would achieve success in his career. But Fulbert proceeded to publicize the marriage. When she denied it, he beat her to try to force her to admit the truth. Abelard heard of this and whisked her away to her childhood convent at Argenteuil.

Fulbert's hatred of Abelard had not abated. Canon law insisted that only entire men could be priests. Knowing this, Fulbert hired a gang of ruffians to castrate Abelard. They accomplished this one night in Abelard's room. His eunuch state brought a despairing Abelard near suicide. Yet he became reconciled to his suffering as the will of God, decided to become a monk, and entered the Abbey of St. Denis. He founded a monastic school known as the Paraclete.

When Abelard was invited to become abbot of St. Gildas-de-Rhuys in Brittany, he handed on Paraclete to Heloise, who had since taken the veil. There she founded her own sisterhood. St. Gildas proved to be a poisoned chalice for Abelard: the worldly and dissolute monks in residence there—some of whom lived openly with their mistresses—resisted Abelard's attempts at disci-

Left: A 14th-century vision of courtly love.

Above: The sepulcher in Père Lachaise cemetery in Paris where Abelard and Heloise now rest.

Right: The croizier—good shepherd's crook and symbol of power—of the abbot of Clairvaux, who instigated the synod of Soissons's charge of heresy against Abelard's teachings.

pline to the point of plotting to assassinate him.

The famous correspondence between Abelard and Heloise began with a beautiful and eloquent plea from Heloise for Abelard to write to her. Abelard's austere response was for the most part a formulaic letter from an abbot to an abbess, full of pious exhortations. But he revealed his true feelings when he asked that, if his enemies killed him, Heloise bury him in the cemetery at the Paraclete. Taking this one paragraph as her cue, Heloise wrote back passionately.

Abelard felt obliged to compose an even more severe letter, extracted here, that warned her of the dangers lying in wait for those who brood longingly over joys that have once been but can never come again, and begged her to accept both God's punishment and forgiveness. After this they continued to correspond on more neutral theological and religious matters. As he had requested in his first letter, his remains were buried at the Paraclete by Heloise, and on her death in 1164, hers were laid beside them. In 1800 their ashes were taken to Paris, and in 1817 they were interred in a single sepulcher, beneath a plinth that reads: "Abelard—Heloise—For Ever One."

MARY, QUEEN OF SCOTS
TO
THE EARL OF BOTHWELL

February 7, 1567

In one of history's famous forgeries, Mary purportedly writes to her lover two days before he murders her husband.

Mary around the age of 16–18. Queen almost from birth, she was the focus of political maneuvers all her life.

James Hepburn, 4th earl of Bothwell (1535–78), Mary's third husband, died insane during his exile in Denmark.

his is the most notorious of the eight "Casket letters" said to have been written by Mary, Queen of Scots. It reinforces the lesson that many of history's famous letters are of doubtful authenticity; research has shown this one to be a forgery.

Mary's first husband, the king of France, died in 1560 when she was 18, and she married her cousin Henry Stewart, Lord Darnley, in 1565. A year later, a jealous Darnley took part in the assassination, before Mary's own eyes, of David Riccio, her secretary and favorite. Mary then suspected Darnley of murderous designs against her and her newborn son James, whom he may have

thought to be Riccio's, and by the end of 1566 divorce was openly discussed.

Darnley spoke of leaving the country but fell ill, probably with syphilis, in Glasgow in January 1567. On the 25th, Mary went to see Darnley, and six days later brought him to Edinburgh. He was lodged in a small mansion beside the Kirk o'Field, just outside the southern walls, where Mary visited him and helped to nurse him.

Between 10 and 11 P.M. on the evening of Sunday, February 9, after some friendly conversation with Darnley, Mary left the house to take part in a masque at Holyrood Palace. About two hours after midnight Darnley's house was blown up with gunpowder. His lifeless body and that of his valet were found in the garden, where they had apparently run just before the explosion, only to be strangled by persons unknown. The chief suspect for leadership of this plot was the Earl of Bothwell. When Bothwell was brought

Biography

Mary, Queen of Scots (1542–87), was the daughter of James V of Scotland by his second wife, Mary of Guise. A grand-niece of Henry VIII, she was in line to the English throne, immediately after Elizabeth I. Promised to Francis, the French dauphin, she spent most of her childhood in France. Francis came to the throne in 1559 and Mary became queen of France at 17, but he died a year later. On her return to Scotland in 1561 she was sucked into a whirlpool of intrigue. A prisoner of Elizabeth I after 1568, she met with great dignity her execution in 1587, accused of complicity in Catholic plots against Elizabeth.

Above: Mary's tapestry monogram.

Opposite, bottom: The "copy" of Mary's letter.

Opposite, top: Mary's pomander, an ornate flower-shaped dispenser for scent, worn on a golden chain.

I watched later up there (Kirk o'Field) than I would have done, had it not been to draw out what this bearer will tell you: that I find the best matter to excuse your affair that could be offered. I have promised him (Darnley) to bring him (her stepbrother) to him (Darnley) tomorrow: if you find it good, put order to it. Now, Sir, I have broken my promise, for you have commanded me not to send or write. Yet I do it not to offend you, and if you know my dread of giving offense you would not have so many suspicions against me, which, none the less, I cherish, as coming from the thing in the world which I most desire and seek, namely your good grace. Of that my conduct shall assure me, nor shall I ever despair thereof, so long as, according to your promise, you lay bare your heart to me. Otherwise I shall think that my misfortune, and the faint attitude of those who have not the third part of the loyalty and willing obedience that I bear to you, have gained over me the advantage won by the second love of Jason.

Not that I compare you to one so unhappy, nor myself to one so pitiless as Medea, however much you make me a little like her in what concerns you; but to preserve and guard you for her to whom alone you belong, if one can appropriate what one gains by honorably, and loyally, and absolutely loving, as I do and will all my life, come what pain and misery there may. I do not ask you to keep promise with me tomorrow, but that we meet and that you do not listen to any suspicion you may have without letting me know. And I ask no more of God than that you may know what is in my heart which is yours, and that He preserve you at least during my life, which shall be dear to me only while my life and I are dear to you. I am going to bed, and wish you good night. Let me know early tomorrow how you fare, for I shall be anxious. And keep good watch if the bird leave his cage, with or without his mate. Like the turtle I shall abide alone, to lament the absence, however short it may be. What I cannot do, my letter would do heartily, if it were not that I fear you are asleep.

Marie R

129

Above: Mary rising to go to her execution while ladies in waiting try to bar her way—painted 232 years later in 1819 by Philippe Jacques van Brée (1786-1871).

to trial and acquitted, suspicion that the queen had known of the plot deepened. Suspicion hardened after her "abduction" by Bothwell on April 24. On May 7, Bothwell divorced the pretty wife he had just married; on the 12th, Mary pardoned the abduction and created Bothwell duke of Orkney and Shetland; and on the 15th—apparently to protect him—she married the man universally regarded as her husband's murderer.

A coalition of Scottish lords now rose in revolt against the scandalous couple, defeating them at Carberry Hill near Edinburgh on June 15, 1567. Mary abdicated in favor of her infant son (James VI of Scotland, later James I of England), with her half brother James Stewart, earl of Moray, as regent.

Ten months later she raised an army against Moray and was defeated again. She fled to England and appealed to Elizabeth I to sustain her claim to Scotland. Elizabeth thought Scotland would be better governed if she controlled it herself, but respected Mary's queenly status. Keeping

Mary under armed guard in Carlisle castle, she prepared a conference (which convened in York in 1568) to adjudicate between Mary and Moray.

The chief evidence was a selection of documents allegedly written by Mary, the so-called "Casket letters." The letter extracted here was purported to prove both Mary's adultery with Bothwell before Darnley's death, and her complicity in his murder. The conference ended with the ludicrous verdict of "not proven": it was held that neither Moray nor Mary had had anything proved against them. Yet one (Mary) remained a prisoner, while the other (Moray) returned to Scotland to rule in her place, virtually a pawn of Elizabeth.

The Casket documents—eight letters, twelve love sonnets, and two marriage contracts—were an ingenious farrago of clever forgeries, fragments of genuine letters, letters from other men's mistresses, and Bothwell's previous love letters. The originals were destroyed—making it impossible to check the telling detail of the handwriting.

The extraordinarily obscure content of this letter suggests either that the copyist found the original difficult to decipher or—more likely—that the original was clumsily forged. Its length makes it implausible that Mary would have written it on February 7, just two days before Darnley's death. At this time Bothwell was in constant attendance on her—why write a long letter of explanation to someone you see every day? The reference to her "misfortune" makes no sense at this stage of Mary's career. The reference to a rival for Bothwell's affections is likewise meaningless. The only candidate as a rival was Bothwell's wife Jean Gordon, yet the writer of the letter compares herself to Medea, the first wife of Jason, whom he deserted to marry Glauce. But the Medea in this case was Jean Gordon and the Glauce, Mary, not the other way

Right: An illuminated prayer book used by Mary, and the golden rosary and crucifix which she wore at her execution.

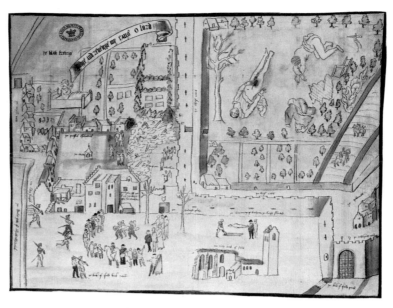

Above: This sketch of how Darnley and his valet were found was made as a record of evidence. Both were in nightshirts, Darnley on his back.

around. The idea that Darnley is the bird who flies out of the cage, while Mary is the dove who mourns his absence, does not make sense either. If Mary were "lamenting" her husband Darnley's absence, the letter stating this could hardly be used—as it was—as evidence that she was planning his murder.

HORATIO NELSON
TO
EMMA, LADY HAMILTON

October 19, 1805

On the eve of his finest victory, the great hero of British naval history writes last words of endearment to his mistress.

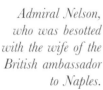

Admiral Nelson, who was besotted with the wife of the British ambassador to Naples.

Emma, who died penniless in France, despite Nelson's dying wishes.

n October 20, 1805, the French admiral Pierre de Villeneuve ventured out of Cadiz harbor, where the British navy had bottled up his combined Franco-Spanish fleet since August, frustrating Napoleon's plans for invading England. The next day, Villeneuve's armada of 34 was engaged off Cape Trafalgar by Horatio Nelson's fleet of 27 British ships. Villeneuve's forces were annihilated in the Royal Navy's greatest-ever triumph. This victory had a price—Nelson's death from musket wounds. On December 4, Nelson's flagship *Victory* brought his body home to Portsmouth. His aide, Captain Hardy, took Nelson's last letters to his mistress Emma, Lady Hamilton, who wrote on receiving them: "This letter was found open upon his desk and brought to Lady Hamilton by Captain Hardy. Oh, miserable, wretched Emma! Oh, glorious and happy Nelson!"

Born Amy Lyon in 1761, the daughter of a Cheshire blacksmith, Emma Hamilton spent her early life in London as a high-class courtesan. In 1782, after many liaisons and an illegitimate child, she accepted the "protection" of Sir William Hamilton, the British ambassador to the kingdom of Naples; they married in 1791. In Naples Emma met Nelson. He had married the widowed Mrs. Frances Nisbet in 1787, but now became besotted with the wife of the British ambassador. His passion was returned, and Nelson and Emma soon became lovers. Sir William Hamilton accepted the situation,

Above: A commemorative mug of the early 1800's.

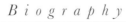

Biography

Horatio Nelson (1758–1805) joined the navy at the age of 12 and rose to the rank of captain by the time he was 20. During the war with Revolutionary France in the 1790's, he played a major part in victories at Toulon (1795) and Cape St. Vincent (1797). The great victory over the French at the Battle of the Nile (1798) set the seal on Nelson's reputation; he was made Baron Nelson of the Nile and granted a pension of £2,000 a year. The King of Naples made him Baron Bronte. Promoted vice admiral in 1801, he won another outstanding victory at Copenhagen in the same year. Nelson capped all his achievements with his victory at Trafalgar in 1805.

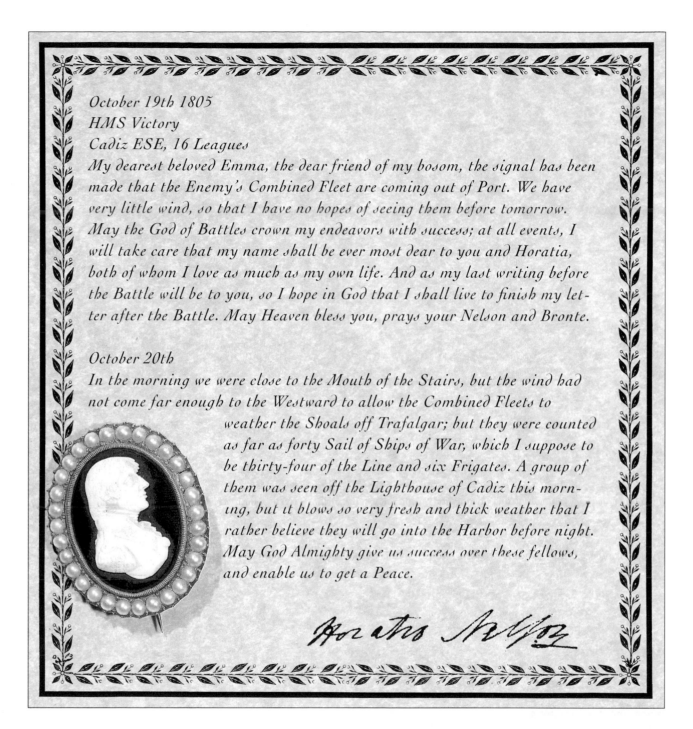

October 19th 1805

HMS Victory

Cadiz ESE, 16 Leagues

My dearest beloved Emma, the dear friend of my bosom, the signal has been made that the Enemy's Combined Fleet are coming out of Port. We have very little wind, so that I have no hopes of seeing them before tomorrow. May the God of Battles crown my endeavors with success; at all events, I will take care that my name shall be ever most dear to you and Horatia, both of whom I love as much as my own life. And as my last writing before the Battle will be to you, so I hope in God that I shall live to finish my letter after the Battle. May Heaven bless you, prays your Nelson and Bronte.

October 20th

In the morning we were close to the Mouth of the Stairs, but the wind had not come far enough to the Westward to allow the Combined Fleets to weather the Shoals off Trafalgar; but they were counted as far as forty Sail of Ships of War, which I suppose to be thirty-four of the Line and six Frigates. A group of them was seen off the Lighthouse of Cadiz this morning, but it blows so very fresh and thick weather that I rather believe they will go into the Harbor before night. May God Almighty give us success over these fellows, and enable us to get a Peace.

Horatio Nelson

Above: A commemorative brooch with Nelson's profile.

Right: A contemporary caricature of Emma's despair on Nelson's departure to fight the French.

but for his sake it was agreed that Nelson and Emma would not openly live together.

In January 1801 Emma bore Nelson a daughter, conceived aboard Nelson's ship the *Foudroyant* in April 1800. Her name, Horatia, was the only obvious sign of her parentage, for Emma concealed the pregnancy. The birth was registered under the paternity of a sailor named Thomson.

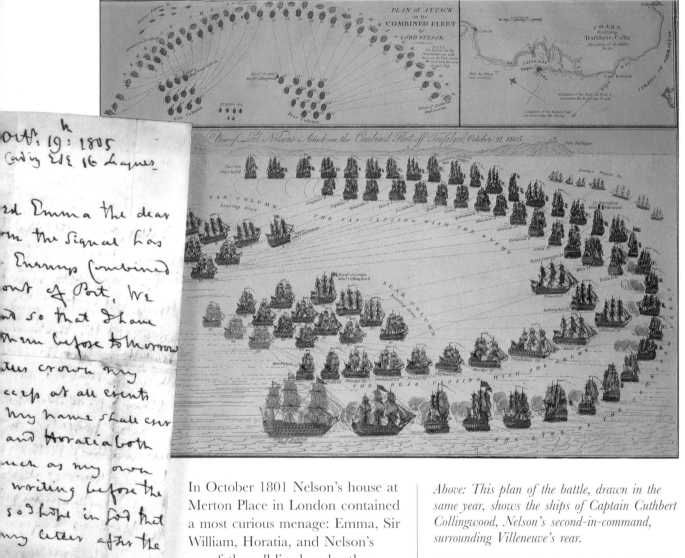

Oct: 19:th 1805
Cadiz E:t E. 16 Leagues

...d Emma the dear...
...n the Signal has...
...Enemys Combined...
...out of Port, We...
...d so that I have...
...them before to morrow...
...ties crown my...
...ccep at all events...
my name shall ever...
...and Horatia both...
...uch as my own...
...writing before the...
...so I hope in God that...
...my letter after the...

In October 1801 Nelson's house at Merton Place in London contained a most curious menage: Emma, Sir William, Horatia, and Nelson's own father all lived under the same roof.

Sir William Hamilton died in 1803. By this time the cult of Nelson (already England's greatest naval hero after his victories at the Nile and Copenhagen) barred the way to Nelson's divorce and remarriage. Although his passion for Emma, rejection of his wife, and cuckolding of Hamilton were plain to see, Nelson insisted on public denials, destroyed all his letters from Emma, and urged her to do the same with his. It was only because Emma disobeyed him that the true facts about their affair are known.

Nelson wrote Emma numerous letters when they were apart. These often demonstrate their deeply passionate relationship. That Emma was constantly in his thoughts is shown by this letter, completed on the eve of the battle of Trafalgar,

Above: This plan of the battle, drawn in the same year, shows the ships of Captain Cuthbert Collingwood, Nelson's second-in-command, surrounding Villeneuve's rear.

Right: While his victorious fleet wins the battle of Trafalgar, Nelson lies on the deck, dying of wounds from musket fire.

the engagement in which Nelson met his death. On the day of the battle, with the enemy fleet in sight, Nelson dictated his will, witnessed by Captains Hardy and Blackwood. He requested that Emma be given an adequate pension to sustain her rank in life. He also left her and Horatia as bequests to the nation; almost his dying words were: "and never forget Horatia." But Emma Hamilton had made many enemies during her scandalous career. She and Horatia were not even invited to Nelson's funeral, and the great sailor-hero's request was ignored. The Prince Regent took an interest in Emma's welfare until a vengeful servant, dismissed from Emma's service,

stole some of Nelson's letters and sold them to the press. The published letters revealed that some years earlier Nelson had warned Emma against the Prince Regent—a notorious philanderer—in language distinctly unflattering to the prince. So ended all hopes of assistance for Emma from the royal purse. By contrast, Nelson's legal and blood relations were treated with

Right: "England slips beneath the waves" is the theme of this wistful French souvenir of the early 1880's. As the hands of the watch turn, the British ship sinks.

largess. Nelson's wife was granted an annual pension of £1,800; his ineffectual brother was granted an earldom, an annual pension of £5,000, and a grant of £100,000 with which to purchase a suitable estate; each of Nelson's sisters received £10,000. Emma, left with just £2,000 a year from the bequests of Nelson and Sir William, soon ran up large bills, which amounted to £18,000 in debt in 1808. She was arrested as a debtor in 1813. On her discharge she fled to Calais, where she spent the last year of her life in poverty and squalor.

Mary Shelley
to
Maria Gisborne

August 15, 1822

The author of Frankenstein *describes
the death of her poet husband, drowned
off the coast of Italy.*

*Mary Shelley, whose Italian
sojourn claimed her husband
and two of their children.*

y boat is swift and beautiful," wrote the English poet Percy Bysshe Shelley in 1822, "and appears quite a vessel. Williams is captain and we drive along this delightful bay in the evening wind, under the summer moon, until earth appears another world." It was in this swift and beautiful schooner, the *Ariel*, that Shelley and his friend Edward Williams met their deaths on July 8, 1822. A sudden storm caught them on their homeward sail across the Gulf of La Spezia; their bodies washed up on the shore eight days later. Shelley was not quite 30.

Shelley's twenties had already been an extraordinary decade of passion, death, flight, and tragedy. He deserted his wife Harriet, and eloped with Mary Godwin, the writer of the letter extracted here. (The letter was to Mary's former nurse, a close friend.) In 1816, when Shelley was 24, Mary gave birth to their first son, William. Her stepsister Claire, who accompanied them on their European travels,

unsuccessfully pursued the poet Lord Byron across Europe, after a brief liaison. Back in London, Harriet drowned herself, and Mary's half-sister Fanny also committed suicide.

Amidst the turmoil, Mary started work on her novel *Frankenstein*, and Shelley produced some of his greatest poetry. The following year, 1817, their daughter, Clara, was born, and Allegra, child of the union between Claire and Byron. Clara died in Venice in 1818 after a fatiguing coach journey. William and Allegra died in Rome not much later. A second son, Percy Shelley, was born in 1819. When Shelley moved his family to a remote house on the beach at San Terenzo near Lerici, on Italy's

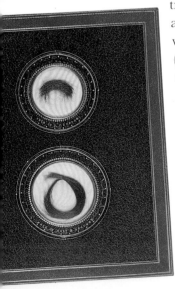

*Left: Locks of hair (Shelley's above and
Mary's below) mounted by a collector in
the leather binding of a copy of Mary's*
Last Days of Percy Bysshe Shelley.

Biography

Mary Wollstonecraft Shelley (1797–1851) was the daughter of the feminist philosopher Mary Wollstonecraft. From the age of 17 her life was bound up with that of the poet Shelley, who was greatly influenced by the political and philosophical views of her father, William Godwin. After Shelley's death Mary edited and published much of his work, and was also a novelist and travel writer. *Frankenstein, or The Modern Prometheus* (1818) was her first novel. Others include *Valperga, Prince of Lucca* (1823), *The Last Man* (1826), *The Fortunes of Perkin Warbeck* (1830), and *Falkner* (1837). Shelley contributed to her *History of a Six Weeks' Tour* (1817), which recounts their earlier travels.

I said that I would send you some account of the last miserable months of my disastrous life. On Monday 8th Jane had a letter from Edward, dated Saturday, he said that he waited at Leghorn for S(helley) who was at Pisa. That S(helley)'s return was certain, "but" he continued, "if he should not come by Monday I will come in a felucca & you may expect me Tuesday evening at furthest." This was Monday, the fatal Monday, but with us it was stormy all day & we did not at all suppose that they could put to sea. Reports were brought us — we hoped — & yet to tell you all the agony we endured during those 12 days would be to make you conceive a universe of pain — each moment intolerable & giving place to one still worse. I said to Jane — "If anything had been found on the coast Trelawny would have returned to let us know. He has not returned so I hope." About 7 o'clock P.M. he did return — all was over — all was quiet now, they had been found washed on shore — Well all this was to be endured.

Today — this day — the sun shining in the sky — they are gone to the desolate sea coast to perform the last offices to their earthly remains. Hunt, L(ord) B(yron) & Trelawny. The quarantine laws would not permit us to remove them sooner — & now only on condition that we burn them to ashes.

I rest now — but soon I must leave Italy — & then — there is an end of all but despair. Adieu. I hope you are well & happy.

Yours ever truly,

Mary S.

northwestern coast, Mary was filled with terrible foreboding. She would say later (1839): "During the whole of our stay in Lerici an intense presentiment of coming evil brooded over my mind, and covered this beautiful place and genial summer with the shadow of coming misery." This seems hardly surprising. By the time Shelley arrived in Lerici in 1822, his European journey seemed strewn with dead children.

Before the fatal boat trip, Shelley had felt disturbed. He dreamed of death and murder. Even so Shelley, with his passion for boats and water, disregarded the storm warnings, and he and Williams met their deaths in a dangerous sea.

Above: Shelley's cremation on the beach where he washed up. Present were the poet Lord Byron, the essayist Leigh Hunt, and the sailor and adventurer Edward Trelawny.

SIMÓN BOLÍVAR
TO
GENERAL FLORES

November 9, 1830

*The liberator of South America writes on his deathbed
to the first president of Ecuador predicting that tyrants
will arise after his death.*

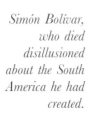

*Simón Bolívar,
who died
disillusioned
about the South
America he had
created.*

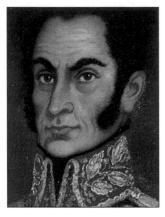

*General Juan
José Flores in
1865, after
helping to fulfill
Bolívar's
prophesy.*

ritten in the last month of Simón Bolívar's life, this letter from the Liberator of South America was both a cry of despair at seeing his life's work in ruins and an accurate forecast of the coming political climate.

Bolívar became a revolutionary after the Venezuelan declaration of independence from Spain in 1811. For the next six years, as Spanish armies triumphed in the wars of independence, Bolívar was reduced to playing a gadfly role from his base in the West Indies. But after 1817 the cause of Latin American autonomy began to make significant progress. As a general, Bolívar won a string of victories—at Boyacá in 1819, at Carabobo in 1821, and at Pichincha in 1822. With the help of General de Sucre, who defeated the Spanish at the battle of Ayacucho (1824),

*In earlier, more hopeful days,
Bolívar planned campaigns
against the Spanish and
wrote rousing calls to the
South American people from
this house in Ciudad Bolívar
(then Angostura), Venezuela.*

he finally expelled the Spanish from South America. Since he had also faced down José de San Martín, the liberator of southern South America, at a meeting at Guayaquil, Ecuador, Bolívar emerged from the wars of independence as the uncrowned king of the American continent south of latitude 15°N.

After 1824 the victors began to fall out among themselves. First the Peruvians rejected Bolívar as their ruler. Then, in 1828, the new country of Bolivia (named after him) expelled Sucre, its first president, and his Colombian troops. When Bolívar assumed dictatorial powers in Colombia in 1828, Venezuela broke away as

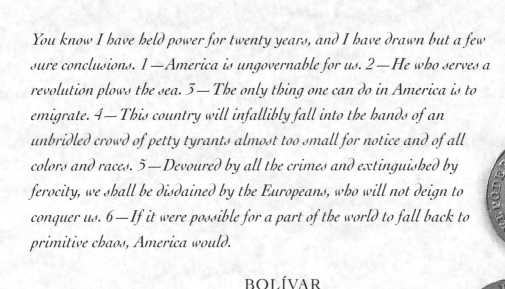

You know I have held power for twenty years, and I have drawn but a few sure conclusions. 1—America is ungovernable for us. 2—He who serves a revolution plows the sea. 3—The only thing one can do in America is to emigrate. 4—This country will infallibly fall into the hands of an unbridled crowd of petty tyrants almost too small for notice and of all colors and races. 5—Devoured by all the crimes and extinguished by ferocity, we shall be disdained by the Europeans, who will not deign to conquer us. 6—If it were possible for a part of the world to fall back to primitive chaos, America would.

BOLÍVAR

well, to become an independent country. In the last year of the Liberator's life the threat of splintering continued, for Colombia itself was now effectively ruled by four regional leaders owing only nominal allegiance to Bolívar in Bogotá.

Bolívar wrote in despair to one of these leaders. Juan José de Flores (1801–64) was a 23-year-old Venezuelan colonel serving in Peru when he came to the Liberator's notice in Lima in 1824. Quickly promoted to the rank of general, Flores was instrumental in having Bolívar proclaimed dictator for life in each conquered city. But Flores had despotic tendencies. When choosing a successor, Bolívar passed him over for Sucre.

Despite his reservations about aspects of Flores's character, Bolívar thought him potentially a great man. Flores proved to be one of those who did rise on Bolívar's tomb; he led a secession movement in southern Colombia, which split off to become the new nation-state of Ecuador, with himself its first president.

Bolívar had dreamed of the states of South America becoming united in a federal system powerful enough to challenge the United States. What he saw at the end of his life was a single country (Colombia) in the process of disintegration. Bolívar proved a true prophet. His death

ushered in 60 years of rule throughout South America by caudillos, the "men on horseback," personal rulers with a military following. The caudillo tradition would continue in South America, strong enough in areas for a wag to nickname the entire region "the land of the long-playing record—33 revolutions a minute."

Above: Ecuadorian currency.

Right: Part of a mural in the Capitol building, Caracas, showing Bolívar's victory at Carabobo.

JOHN BROWN
TO
HIS FAMILY

November 30, 1859

*Strengthened in his faith by the courage
of his convictions, the renowned abolitionist
comforts his family shortly before his execution.*

*John Brown, waiting the
hour of his execution "with
great composure of mind."*

On October 16, 1859, John Brown, the fiery abolitionist, and his men (five of them black) seized the federal arsenal at Harpers Ferry, Virginia, as the first step in a hoped-for slave insurrection. "One man and God can overturn the universe," Brown declared. The next day Col. Robert E. Lee (later the Confederate Civil War general) arrived with a company of United States Marines from Washington. Brown and six of his men barricaded themselves in an engine-house and fought until two of his sons were killed and he himself was severely wounded.

Tried by a Virginia court for slave insurrection, treason, and murder, he was convicted and hanged at Charles Town, Virginia, along with four of his men (two more were executed later). Seated on his own coffin while he rode in a wagon to the

*Left: Antislavery image
from a Wedgwood
cameo of the 1830's.*

gallows, Brown gazed at the Blue Ridge Mountains and remarked: "This *is* a beautiful country, I never had the pleasure of really seeing it before." After the hanging, the jailer unfolded a slip of paper on which Brown left a prophetic message: "I, John Brown, am now quite *certain* that the crimes of this *guilty* land will never be purged *away* but with Blood."

Brown is one of the most controversial figures in American history. To detractors, and to some abolitionists, he was a fanatic, a religious maniac who focused his madness on the issue of slavery. To his admirers, he was a saint, a man who even in the shadow of death refused to implicate his collaborators among the northern abolitionists.

Biography

John Brown (1800–59) was born in Torrington, Connecticut, of Pilgrim descent. A biblical-style patriarch, he married twice and had 20 children. In the Kansas border conflict of 1854–56, central to which was the larger national struggle over slavery, Brown established himself as a self-proclaimed leader of the fight to end slavery. He became notorious for the massacre at Pottawatomie Creek in Kansas, when he and four of his sons attacked and killed five proslavery men with broadswords. He struck fear into the hearts of the South when he set up a stronghold and refuge for runaway slaves. His attack on the Harpers Ferry arsenal in 1859 led to his capture and execution.

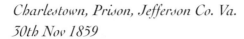

Charlestown, Prison, Jefferson Co. Va.
30th Nov 1859
My Dearly beloved Wife, Sons: & Daughters,
As I now begin what is probably the last letter I shall ever
write to any of you; I conclude to write you all at the same time.
I am waiting the hour of my public murder with great composure of
mind, & cheerfulness: feeling the strongest assurance that in no other possible
way could I be used to so much advance the cause of God; & of humanity: The reflection
that a wise, & merciful, as well as Just, & holy God: rules not only the affairs of this
world; but of all the worlds; is a rock to set our feet upon; under all circumstances: I have
now no doubt but that our seeming disaster: will ultimately result in the most glorious
success. So my dear shattered; & broken family; be of good cheer; &
believe & trust in God; I beseech you every one to make the bible your
daily & nightly study; with a childlike honest, candid, teachable
spirit: out of love and respect for your Husband; & Father; & I
beseech the God of my Fathers; to open all your eyes to a discovery of
the truth. John Brown writes to his children to abhor with undying
hatred, also: that "sum of all villainies" Slavery. Remember that "he
that is slow to anger is better than the mighty: and he that ruleth his
spirit; than he that taketh a city." Remember also: that "they that
be wise shall shine: and they that turn many to righteousness: as the
stars forever; & ever." And now dearly beloved Farewell. To God &
the word of his grace I commend you all.
Your Affectionate Husband & Father

JOHN BROWN

Top: Slave manacles of the 1840's.

Above: "The Last Moments of John Brown," painted by Thomas Hovenden (1840-95).

The song "John Brown's body lies a-moldering in the grave" was popular with Union soldiers during the Civil War, and Harpers Ferry may have made conflict between North and South inevitable rather than just probable.

Brown's letter to his family, abridged above, is a typical utterance, full of biblical imagery and Old Testament sensibility. He was known for larding his speech with scriptural references; when taking his sons out into the Kansas wilderness in 1854 he had exhorted them to trust in God to provide for their bodily needs, as the Lord God Jehovah had fed the prophet Elijah through the ravens. Brown himself has often been likened to an Old Testament prophet. He railed against the "peculiar institution" of slavery with all the vehemence of the biblical prophets in the face of idolatry and polytheism. Clearly, in Brown's mind, to die fighting against the evil of slavery was a worthy martyrdom.

ABRAHAM LINCOLN
TO
MRS. LYDIA BIXBY

November 21, 1864

At the height of the Civil War,
President Lincoln finds time to write a moving
letter of condolence to a bereaved mother.

Abraham Lincoln, who was
not correctly informed about
Mrs. Bixby's sons.

he American Civil War (1861–65) produced casualties on a scale that had not been seen in warfare since the Thirty Years War in Europe (1618–48). Out of a population of 21 million, the casualties (dead and wounded) were well over a million. In the North 2 million combatants suffered 640,000 casualties, while in the South 450,000 casualties occurred out of 750,000 troops. The total death toll from the war (including not just deaths in battle but related phenomena such as drowning, sunstroke, execution, suicide, and above all, disease) was 621,000 (365,000 Federals and 256,000 Confederates). These figures from a four-year war gain added significance when compared with 20 years of European warfare in the Napoleonic era that produced little more than a million dead.

In fact, the American Civil War was the transition into modern war—the use of repeating rifles and primitive machine guns raised the technology of killing to unprecedented heights. It was also a war waged with remarkable ruthlessness. Gen. William Sherman's "scorched earth" policy in Georgia tore the heart out of the Confederacy in 1864. Gen. Philip Sheridan's methods, anticipating those of Gen. George Patton in World War II, so devastated the Shenandoah Valley in 1864 that it was said that a crow flying over the area would have to carry its own rations to survive.

In the midst of this carnage, the repeated solicitude of President Lincoln for the losses of his acquaintances stands in poignant contrast. In 1862 he dispatched letters to the daughters of two victims of the Vicksburg campaign, and with his own son Willie not long dead, Lincoln also understood a parent's grief. His deep human sympathy led him to reach out beyond his personal circle, and this letter to Lydia Bixby, a Boston widow, is the most famous instance. The fact that he had been misinformed (only two of

Biography

Abraham Lincoln (1809–65), 16th president of the United States, was born in Kentucky, grew up in Indiana, and became a lawyer (entirely self-educated) in Illinois. Elected to the state legislature in 1834, he became a congressman in 1846. When the Republican party was organized in 1856 to oppose the extension of slavery, Lincoln headed the Illinois caucus. His famous debates on slavery with Senator Stephen Douglas in 1858 led the party to select him as Republican candidate for the presidency in 1860. His election precipitated the Civil War. Five days after the South surrendered, Lincoln was assassinated by John Wilkes Booth while attending the theater in Washington.

Executive Mansion
Washington, Nov. 21, 1864

To Mrs. Bixby, Boston, Mass.

Dear Madam,

I have been shown in the files of the War Department a statement of the Adjutant-General of Massachusetts that you are the mother of five sons who have died gloriously on the field of battle. I feel how weak and fruitless must be any word of mine which should attempt to beguile you from the grief of a loss so overwhelming. But I cannot refrain from tendering you the consolation that may be found in the thanks of the republic they died to save. I pray that our Heavenly Father may assuage the anguish of your bereavement, and leave you only the cherished memory of the loved and lost, and the solemn pride that must be yours to have laid so costly a sacrifice upon the altar of freedom.

Yours very sincerely and respectfully,

A. Lincoln

Mrs. Bixby's sons were killed in action; of the other three, two deserted and one was honorably discharged) does not detract from the purity of Lincoln's motives or from his humanity.

The authenticity of this letter has sometimes been questioned, largely because so many clever facsimiles exist. Some people have alleged that it was written not by Lincoln but by his secretary John Hay. However, the very best scholarship has established it as genuine. Despite attempts to discredit the letter on grounds of authorship, authenticity, and wrong information, it soars above all criticism to remain one of the truly noble expressions of condolence in world literature.

Above: Memorabilia of war: new photographic techniques in the 1860's meant soldiers could now send portraits home.

VINCENT VAN GOGH
TO
THEO VAN GOGH

July 24, 1890

*The letter found in the artist's pocket
after he shoots himself tells of
his brother's role in his life and art.*

*Self-portrait, by
Vincent van
Gogh, painted in
1889, the last
of many that
he produced.*

*Theo van Gogh,
the artist's
brother, who
survived Vincent
by only six
months.*

On the afternoon of Sunday, July 27, 1890, the 37-year-old Vincent van Gogh left his lodgings at Auvers-sur-Oise, a village 20 miles north of Paris. Unusually for him, he was not carrying a canvas and a passer-by later noticed him sitting in a tree muttering: "It is impossible, impossible." He returned a few hours later and lay down quietly, asking to be left alone. His landlady, seeing blood on his clothes, called for his friend and doctor, Paul Gachet. When he arrived, Vincent said: "I think I've bungled it; what do you say?" A bullet from a borrowed revolver had entered his chest and stomach. He lasted for two days and died with his brother Theo at his side, still lucid enough to indicate that he had shot himself while in full control of his faculties and not in a fit. Suicidal tendencies and a fascination with death had marked Vincent's career from his early twenties. When his father died in 1885 Vincent said: "It is easier for me to die than to live. Dying is hard but living is still harder." His painting, "The Empty Chair," was inspired by the story that the English artist Luke Fildes had drawn Charles

Dickens's chair the morning after the novelist's death. In the notes to his famous painting "Starry Night," with whorls of light so intense they seem almost within reach, van Gogh writes: "Why, I ask myself, shouldn't the shining dots of the sky be as accessible as the black dots on the map of France? Just as we take a train to reach Tarascon or Rouen, we take death to reach a star."

Probably it was fear of losing Theo that precipitated the final breakdown. There was a curious symbiosis between the two brothers. Events in the life of one would trigger, almost unconsciously, a reaction in the other. Vincent once told Theo: "If I did not have your friendship, I should

---

Biography

Vincent van Gogh (1853-90), the son of a Dutch Lutheran pastor, joined Goupil's, the art dealers, and worked for them in London, Paris and The Hague. After his dismissal from the company Vincent studied theology and was an itinerant preacher in the Belgian coalfields before devoting his life to art. Despite continual rejections and disastrous love affairs, he created a series of artistic masterpieces, all painted in the last five years of his life. After an attempt to found an artists' colony at Arles, and a bitter quarrel with fellow artist Paul Gauguin, Vincent sank into depression and was admitted to a mental hospital. Eventually he killed himself in despair.

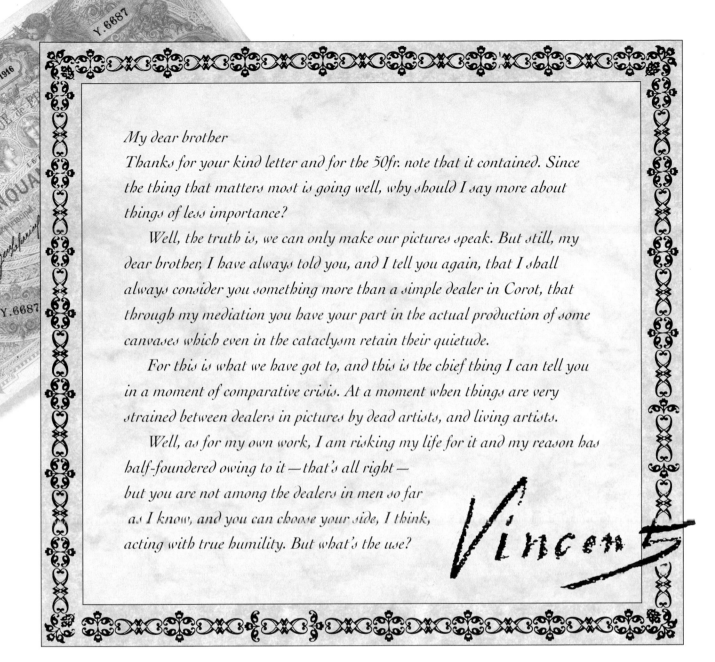

My dear brother

Thanks for your kind letter and for the 50fr. note that it contained. Since the thing that matters most is going well, why should I say more about things of less importance?

Well, the truth is, we can only make our pictures speak. But still, my dear brother, I have always told you, and I tell you again, that I shall always consider you something more than a simple dealer in Corot, that through my mediation you have your part in the actual production of some canvases which even in the cataclysm retain their quietude.

For this is what we have got to, and this is the chief thing I can tell you in a moment of comparative crisis. At a moment when things are very strained between dealers in pictures by dead artists, and living artists.

Well, as for my own work, I am risking my life for it and my reason has half-foundered owing to it — that's all right — but you are not among the dealers in men so far as I know, and you can choose your side, I think, acting with true humility. But what's the use?

Vincent

be remorselessly driven to suicide, and, cowardly as I am, I should commit it in the end." On another occasion he indicated that Theo was his alter ego and in some ways responsible for his life: "A wife you cannot give me, a child you cannot give me. Money, yes."

In 1888 Theo fell in love. This posed a financial threat to Vincent, who was utterly dependent on Theo's generosity. Worse, the love affair faced Vincent with a psychological challenge because of his own many failures with women. Theo's son, who was also christened Vincent, later believed that it was his parents' marriage—and his own birth—that had ultimately killed his uncle. The quarrel between Vincent and the painter Paul Gauguin, which culminated in Vincent cutting off his earlobe, occurred immediately after Vincent heard from Theo that he intended to marry. The marriage itself brought on another crisis, as did the announcement that the baby was expected, and the child's birth.

Many opinions have been expressed as to whether Vincent suffered from a physical disorder that might have led to psychological disturbance: alcoholism, epilepsy, schizophrenia, and Ménière's disease have all been suggested. The most likely diagnosis is that of depressive neurosis, coupled

with psychotic episodes triggered by stress.

There were many bizarre aspects of Vincent's psyche, as is evident from his many letters and revealing notebooks; but his essential lifeline was his relationship with his brother Theo, the only person fully convinced of his genius. The letter abstracted here, found undated and unsigned in Vincent's pocket, may have been a first draft of the letter he had sent to Theo a few days before he shot himself. Its first two sentences are almost identical. Vincent may have decided not to post this draft as it implicitly criticized his brother and showed some resentment at a request for economies.

It is not clear whether the letter deals with emotional or practical anxieties. The mentions of "cataclysm" and "crisis" may relate to suicide, but they might equally refer to the fear that Theo would be dismissed from his job at Goupil's, the art dealers and supporters of many Impressionists. Vincent, who exhibited few paintings in his life and never sold one, felt frustrated that the art market still favored Old Masters over contemporary artists, and celebrated living artists who produced pretty, realistic pictures, leaving no room for work as deeply felt as his own. His disastrous stay at Arles with Gauguin was prompted by the desire to create a community of artists, supporting each other in the hostile climate of late 19th-century France.

Like so much else in Vincent's life, his suicide raises old questions about the role of insanity in the creativity of an artist. Roman philosopher

Left: "Road with a Cypress and a Star" (May 1890). Cypress trees, often resembling flames, and perhaps symbolizing death, were a regular theme in Vincent's work.

Right: The letter found in the dead Vincent's pocket was three pages long.

Seneca said there was no genius without a hint of madness. Psycho-analyst Anna Freud declared that Vincent's tale illustrated a universal truth: even the most highly prized forms of creativity might not give sufficient outlets for the internal conflicts and self-destructiveness that were likely to accompany that creativity.

It was not for another 10 years that Vincent's paintings won wider appreciation, but his passion, vision and honesty found a growing public until his art became the most sought-after in history. Theo, for his part, went mad after Vincent's death and died six months later. The brothers were eventually buried side by side in the graveyard at Auvers.

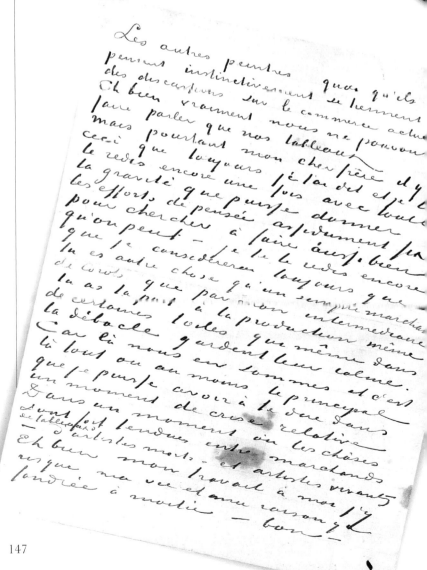

CAPTAIN ROBERT FALCON SCOTT
TO
J. M. BARRIE

March, 1912

*The dying Antarctic explorer asks
his friend to look after his family and the families
of those who are perishing with him.*

*Captain R. F.
Scott, whose
letters snatched
a posthumous
literary victory
from his defeat
at the Pole.*

*J. M. Barrie, the
man who would
write* Peter Pan,
*was the godfather
of Scott's
fatherless son.*

In March 1912 three starving, exhausted men huddled in their tent in the extreme cold of a polar storm in Antarctica. Two other members of the British expedition to reach the South Pole had already died. As Capt. Robert Falcon Scott, the expedition's leader, awaited his own death and that of his companions, he wrote a series of letters to his relatives, friends, and patrons. The letters show the courage with which these men faced their end, the view Scott himself held of their heroism, and above all his concern for the welfare of their families. In his letter to the Scottish novelist and playwright J. M. Barrie (1860–1937), best remembered as the creator of Peter Pan, Scott twice asks his friend

*Top: Snow goggles from Scott's
1901–04 Antarctic expedition.*

*Left: The boots Scott wore
when he commanded the
1901–04 expedition.*

Barrie to look after his wife and son.

Captain Scott, with four companions (Bowers, Evans, Oates, and Wilson), reached the South Pole by an overland route from the Ross Sea on January 17, 1912. Only then did they discover that the rival Norwegian expedition, commanded by Roald Amundsen, had already won the race, having arrived on December 14. Amundsen was thus the first-known human to stand at the South Pole. The secret of Amundsen's success was meticulous planning, superb organization, and a lifetime spent in the polar regions. He was the ultimate professional, the polar explorer's explorer. Scott, by contrast an enthusiastic amateur,

---

Biography

Robert Falcon Scott (1868–1912) commanded the British Antarctic expedition of 1901–04, proving himself to be a good scientific investigator and leader. With Dr. Edward Wilson and Ernest Shackleton, Scott traveled overland toward the South Pole as far as latitude 82°S. In 1910 Scott (who had been promoted to the rank of captain in 1906) set out on a scientific, exploratory expedition aimed at studying the Ross Sea and reaching the Pole. On the return journey, delayed both by unexpectedly bad weather and by the sickness of Edgar Evans, his entire party perished. Scott's epitaph, taken from Tennyson's poem *Ulysses*, sums him up: "To strive, to seek, to find and not to yield."

My Dear Barrie,

We are pegging out in a very comfortless spot. Hoping this letter may be found and sent to you, I write a word of farewell . . . . More practically I want you to help my widow and my boy—your godson. We are showing that Englishmen can still die with a bold spirit, fighting it out to the end. It will be known that we have accomplished our object in reaching the Pole, and that we have done everything possible, even to sacrificing ourselves in order to save sick companions. I think this makes an example for Englishmen of the future, and that the country ought to help those who are left behind to mourn us. I leave my poor girl and your godson, Wilson leaves a widow, and Edgar Evans also a widow in humble circumstances. Do what you can to get their claims recognized. Goodbye. I am not at all afraid of the end, but sad to miss many a humble pleasure which I had planned for the future on our long marches. I may not have proved a great explorer, but we have done the greatest march ever made and come very near to great success. Goodbye, my dear friend,

Yours ever,

R Scott

We are in a desperate state, feet frozen, etc. No fuel and a long way from food, but it would do your heart good to be in our tent, to hear our songs and the cheery conversation as to what we will do when we get to Hut Point.

Later We are very near the end, but have not and will not lose our good cheer. We have had four days of storm in our tent and nowhere's food or fuel. We did intend to finish ourselves when things proved like this, but we have decided to die naturally in the track.

As a dying man, my dear friend, be good to my wife and child. Give the boy a chance in life if the State won't do it. He ought to have good stuff in him . . . . I never met a man in my life whom I admired and loved more than you, but I never could show you how much your friendship meant to me, for you had much to give and I nothing.

Above: A painting by Wilson, who died with Scott.

Below: A gas cooking stove and food rations (beef extract and sugar) from Scott's earlier expedition.

made many mistakes. Scott had made painfully slow progress to the Pole; motor sleds broke down and ponies were used to pull sleds, as opposed to Amundsen's sled dogs. Even worse, Scott had not stored enough food in the depots laid down on the way to the Pole, with the result that on the return journey he and his men literally began to starve to death. Amundsen, traveling twice as fast between depots placed closer together, allowed three times as much cooking fuel and an allowance of 5,500 calories a day. On the return journey Scott, whose ponies had already died and who was physically hauling the sleds, had food depots that were too small, too few, and too far apart. He had placed them on the assumption of animal transportation,

Above:
A picture the party took at the South Pole. Standing: Wilson, Scott, and Bowers. Seated: Evans and Oates.

Right: "Southern Journal, Volume II," Scott's diary, from which he tore pages to write his last letters.

and he had allowed 3,700 calories a day when he needed 6,000. Worst of all, he and his men had no adequate protection against the cold at the time they began to suffer from scurvy, which is caused by deficiency of vitamin C. Scurvy has the effect of destroying tissue, so all their old scars and wounds opened and began to bleed. Scott's party experienced conditions no worse than those endured by Amundsen on his return journey, but they were so weak they could scarcely move their sleds and took nine hours to travel seven miles.

Evans died first, and Oates soon afterward left the tent to meet his death in a blizzard. On March 21, just 11 miles from One Ton Depot, the three survivors huddled in a tent for several days as the elements roared outside. In the letters he wrote at this time, Scott snatched a kind of victory from the jaws of defeat. By playing down the shortcomings of the expedition and not acknowledging his own mismanagement, and elaborating instead the themes of pain, sacrifice, duty, and moral fiber, Scott turned his flawed performance as a polar explorer into an epic of heroism. When Scott's body, diaries, and last letters were found by a search party eight months later, he became the greatest hero of the Edwardian age. A posthumous knighthood was granted to Scott's widow, and his faults forgotten in a blaze of patriotic propaganda that went unchallenged for 70 years. Scott became the heroic failure *par excellence*, while Amundsen was vilified for his "treachery" and failure to "play the game." Scott's final letters are a good example of how literary talent can change the way we perceive the past. Instead of being recognized as an amateur matched against a professional, he acquired the reputation of an angel of light pitted against a prince of darkness. In his lifetime, Amundsen's reputation never recovered from the effects of British image-making.

CARL JUNG
TO
SIGMUND FREUD

December 18, 1912

Jung writes a highly critical letter to his "father Freud" that puts an end to their six-year friendship.

In the front row at a 1909 psychology conference at Clark University, Freud (left) and Jung (right).

 ometimes called the Copernicus of the Mind, the Austrian Sigmund Freud (1856–1939) revolutionized psychology by his discovery of the role of the subconscious in neurosis. His theory postulated that the primary drive in human beings is sexual energy or libido, and that when sexual desires are repressed (forced to remain unconscious), this can lead to neurosis.

In this work lay both the seeds of his fruitful association with another great student of psychology, Carl Gustav Jung, and the forces that would push them apart. Jung, a young Swiss psychiatrist, was among the first people outside Vienna to use psychoanalytic ideas. Jung was prepared to apply these ideas to psychosis (madness), and not just neurosis (mental illness). In 1906–07

Above: The famous couch in Freud's study, from which reclining patients confided their secret conflicts.

Jung published *The Psychology of Dementia Praecox*, a psychoanalytic study of schizophrenia. Freud greeted the book with enthusiasm, and there followed six years of close collaboration. Jung even accompanied Freud to the United States on a lecture tour in 1909.

A delighted Freud spoke of Jung as the "crown prince" of psychoanalysis, and behaved toward him as father to son (Freud was the elder by 19 years). But as sons often rebel against their fathers, so Jung began to turn away from Freud. Jung became disillusioned when Freud refused to submit to analysis himself lest it weaken his

Biography

*C*arl Gustav Jung (1875–1961) studied medicine at the universities of Basel and Zurich, then specialized in psychiatry. In 1907 he began six years of collaboration with Sigmund Freud, a relationship that ended dramatically. His book *The Psychology of the Unconscious* (1911–12) made clear the differences between Freudian psychoanalysis and "analytical psychology," as he termed his own approach. Jung spent many years as a therapist, particularly of middle-aged people whose lives had lost their meaning. He developed ideas of personality types, of archetypes and the collective unconscious, and of the nature of religion. He was professor in Zurich (1933–41) and Basel (1943).

May I say a few words to you in earnest? I admit the ambivalence of my feelings toward you, but am inclined to take an honest and absolutely straightforward view of the situation. If you doubt my word, so much the worse for you. I would, however, point out that your technique of treating your pupils like patients is a blunder. In that way you produce either slavish sons or impudent puppies. I am objective enough to see through your little trick. You go around sniffing out all the symptomatic actions in your vicinity, thus reducing everyone to the level of sons and daughters who blushingly admit the existence of their faults. Meanwhile you remain on top as the father, sitting pretty. For sheer obsequiousness nobody dare pluck the prophet by the beard.

I have submitted lege artis et tout humblement to analysis and am much the better for it. You know, of course, how far a patient gets with self-analysis: not out of his neurosis — just like you. If ever you should rid yourself entirely of your complexes and stop playing the father to your sons, and instead of aiming continually at their weak spots took a good look at your own for a change, then I will mend my ways and at one stroke uproot the vice of being in two minds about you. I shall continue to stand by you publicly while maintaining my own views, but privately shall start telling you in my letters what I really think of you.

No doubt you will be outraged by this peculiar token of friendship, but it may do you good all the same.

With best regards,
Most sincerely, yours,

C. G. Jung

Right: A page from Jung's diary of his dreams, with his "inner voice."

authority. At the same time Freud, who thought religion a neurotic illusion, expressed concern that Jung was trying to find a substitute for the Christian faith he had lost in his youth.

Their intellectual differences came to a head in part because Jung wanted to redefine libido to mean creative energy, not just sexual energy. There were also profound currents of personal conflict between the two men. In fact Freud's career was littered with broken friendships, and there is some truth in Jung's accusation that Freud treated his followers like patients. Jung's letter of December 1912, abstracted above, effectively ended the friendship. These two remarkable men subsequently went very different ways in their careers and, after 1913, never saw each other again.

D. H. LAWRENCE
TO
BERTRAND RUSSELL

February 19, 1916

*Lawrence urges Russell to abandon the
academic life and live not by thinking
but by feeling.*

*David Herbert
Lawrence,
novelist and poet,
who believed in
the supremacy of
instinctual
feelings.*

*Bertrand Russell,
mathematician
and philosopher,
who looked to
reason as the
guiding light in
human affairs.*

D. H. Lawrence and Bertrand Russell met in February 1915. Lawrence had established his reputation as the author of *The White Peacock* (1911) and *Sons and Lovers* (1913). Russell, a world-famous logician, had published (with A. N. Whitehead) a three-volume work called *Principia Mathematica*. The two men had dramatically differing views. Russell sent the draft of a book about politics to Lawrence, who profoundly disagreed with its moderate proposals—paradoxically, Russell, an earl's son, believed in democracy; Lawrence, a miner's son, in autocracy. He returned the manuscript full of corrections. Undaunted, Russell sent a political essay, entitled *The Danger to Civilization*. Lawrence sent an angry response, alleging that Russell's pacifism was really a disguised form of blood-lust: "Your basic desire is the maximum desire of war, you are really the super-war spirit. . . . Let us become strangers again. I think it is better."

Russell at first thought Lawrence had divined unconscious motives of which he (Russell) was

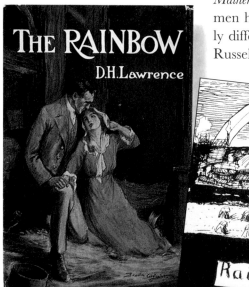

Above: Lawrence's book
The Rainbow, *for which his publishers were
prosecuted under the obscenity laws. The drawing is his.*

Biography

David Herbert Lawrence (1885–1930) was born in Eastwood, Nottinghamshire, and studied at University College, Nottingham. He trained as a schoolmaster and then began to write. An affair with Frieda Weekley, whose husband had taught him at the university, led to her divorce and remarriage to Lawrence in 1914. Despite ill health from tuberculosis, Lawrence wrote prolifically. His major works included 14 novels, poetry, short stories, plays, travel books, and other works on literature, history, and psychology. His work aroused considerable controversy, culminating in an obscenity case in 1960 over the posthumous publication of his last novel, *Lady Chatterley's Lover*.

My dear Russell,

I didn't like your letter. What's the good of living as you do, anyway. I don't believe your lectures are good. One must be an outlaw these days, not a teacher or preacher. One must retire out of the herd and then fire bombs into it. You said in your lecture on education that you didn't set much count by the unconscious. That is sheer perversity. The whole of the consciousness and the conscious content is old hat—the millstone round your neck. Even your mathematics are only dead truth: and no matter how fine you grind the dead meat, you'll not bring it to life again. Do stop working and writing altogether and become a creature instead of a mechanical instrument. Do clear out of the whole social ship. Do for your very pride's sake become a mere nothing, a mole, a creature that feels its way and doesn't think. Do for heavens sake be a baby, and not a savant any more. Don't do anything any more—but for heavens sake begin to be—start at the very beginning and be a perfect baby: in the name of courage. Soon I shall be penniless, and they'll shove me into munitions, and I shall tell 'em what I think of 'em, and end my days in prison or a madhouse. But I don't care. One can still write bombs. But I don't want to be penniless and at their mercy. Life is very good of itself, and I am terrified lest they should get me into their power. They seem to me like an innumerable host of rats, and once they get the scent, one is lost. My love to you. Stop working and being an ego, and have the courage to be a creature.

D H Lawrence

"YOUR COUNTRY NEEDS YOU"

unaware: "For twenty-four hours," he wrote, "I thought I was not fit to live, and contemplated committing suicide." The two men continued to correspond, Lawrence urging Russell, as in the letter abbreviated here, to give up his way of life and thinking. Russell later wrote: "Lawrence is one of a long line of people, beginning with Heraclitus and ending with Hitler, whose ruling motive is hatred derived from megalomania."

Above: A World War I recruitment poster, and men setting off to fight. Lawrence and Russell were united in their common opposition to war, and Russell was later imprisoned as a conscientious objector.

Acknowledgments (Text)

ENCOUNTERS & DISCOVERIES

SAINT JEROME: *A Select Library of Nicene and Post-Nicene Fathers of the Christian Church. Vol. VI, St. Jerome: Letters and Select Works.* James Parker. 1893, Oxford.

KUYUK, MONGOL KHAN: *Mongol Empire.* Michael Prawdin. 1940, Allen & Unwin.

CHRISTOPHER COLUMBUS: *Christopher Columbus. His Life, his Work, his Remains. Vol. 2.* John Boyd Thacher. 1903, G. P. Putnam, London.

HERNANDO PIZARRO: *Reports on the Discovery of Peru.* Clements Markham. 1947, Hakluyt Society.

GALILEO GALILEI: *Journal of History on Astronomy, Vol. 7, Part 3*, pp. 153–68. M. A. Hoskin. 1976, Science History Publications Ltd. By kind permission of Prof. Stillman Drake, Toronto, Canada.

SAMUEL PEPYS: *Samuel Pepys' Letters and the Second Diary, 1656–1703.* Edited by R. G. Howarth. 1932, J. M. Dent and Sons Ltd., London and Toronto.

BENJAMIN FRANKLIN: *Mr. Franklin, a Selection from his Personal Letters.* Edited by Leonard W. Labaree and Whitfield J. Bell, Jr. 1956, Yale University Press, New Haven.

THE COMTE DE BOUGAINVILLE: *The Fatal Impact.* Alan Moorhead. 1966, Reprint Society, London.

QIANLONG, EMPEROR OF CHINA: *The Collision of Two Civilisations, the British Expedition to China, 1792–4.* Alain Peyrefitte, translated by Jon Rothschild. 1992, Collins Harvill, an imprint of HarperCollins Publishers Limited, London.

COMMODORE M. C. PERRY: *A Report of the Secretary of the Navy, in Compliance with a Resolution of the Senate of December 6, 1854 calling for Correspondence Relative to the Naval Expedition to Japan.* 33rd Congress, 2nd session. Ex. Doc. No. 34.

HENRY MORTON STANLEY: *New York Herald*, 1875.

LOUIS PASTEUR: *The Life of Pasteur. Vol. 2.* René Vallery-Radot, translated by Mrs. R.L. Devonshire. 1902, Constable, London.

ALBERT EINSTEIN: *Einstein, the First 100 Years.* Edited by Maurice Goldsmith, Alan Mackay and James Woudhuysen. 1980, Pergammon Press.

SELF-PORTRAITS & JUSTIFICATIONS

DANTE: *The Letters of Dante*, 2nd edition. Edited by Paget Toynbee. 1966. By permission of Oxford University Press, Oxford.

LEONARDO DA VINCI: Original Andromeda translation.

MARTIN LUTHER: *Luther's Works, Vol. 31, Career of the Reformer: 1.* Harold J. Grimm. 1957, Muhlenberg Press (Concordia). Used by permission of Augsburg Fortress.

ANNE BOLEYN: *Letters and Papers, Foreign and Domestic, of the Reign of Henry VIII, Vol. X.* Edited by James Gairdner. 1965, Kraus Reprint, Vaduz, USA.

BONNIE PRINCE CHARLIE: Royal Windsor Archives, Windsor. By gracious permission of Her Majesty the Queen.

GEORGE WASHINGTON: *Treasury of the World's Greatest Letters.* M. Lincoln Schuster. 1948, Simon and Schuster, New York.

MARIE ANTOINETTE: Original Andromeda translation.

THOMAS ALVA EDISON: From the collection of Henry Ford Museum, Greenfield Village, Dearborn, Michigan.

WILLIAM RANDOLPH HEARST: *William Randolph Hearst, American.* Edited by Mrs Fremont Older. 1936, Appleton-Century Company Inc., New York.

VIRGINIA STEPHEN: The Monks House Papers. University of Sussex Library, Brighton.

BARTOLOMEO VANZETTI: *The Letters of Sacco and Vanzetti.* Edited by Marion D. Frankfurter and Gardner Jackson. 1929, Constable, London.

POLICY & CHALLENGES

SAINT PAUL: *New English Bible.* © Oxford University Press and Cambridge University Press 1961, 1970.

PLINY THE YOUNGER: Reprinted by permission of the publishers and the Loeb Classical Library from *Pliny the Younger: Letters and Panegyricus, Vol. II.* Translated by Betty Radice. 1969, Harvard University Press, Cambridge, Mass.

JOAN OF ARC: Original Andromeda translation.

LORENZO DE' MEDICI: *Lives of the Early Medici as Told in their Correspondence.* Translated and edited by Janet Ross. 1910, Chatto and Windus, London.

SIR FRANCIS WALSINGHAM: *Francis Drake.* John Sugden. 1990, Barrie and Jenkins. Original held by Public Record Office, Richmond, Surrey, England.

LOUIS XIV: Original Andromeda translation.

NAPOLEON BONAPARTE: *Letters of Napoleon.* J. M. Thompson. © Basil Blackwell, Oxford, 1934.

ROBERT E. LEE: *Documents of American History, Vol. 1 to 1898*, 19th edition. Henry Steele Commager and Milton Cantor. 1988, Prentice Hall, New Jersey.

KARL MARX:.

ÉMILE ZOLA: *The Dreyfus Case: A Documentary History.* Edited by Louis L. Snyder. Copyright © 1973 by Rutgers University, the State University of New Jersey. Reprinted by permission of Rutgers University Press.

NEVILLE CHAMBERLAIN: *The Struggle for Peace.* Neville Chamberlain. 1939, Hutchinson, London. By kind permission of the Estate of Chamberlain and Random House U.K.

JOHN MAYNARD KEYNES: Unpublished writings of J. M. Keynes. © The Provost and Scholars of King's College, Cambridge, 1993.

WINSTON CHURCHILL: Reproduced with permission of Curtis Brown Ltd, London, on behalf of the Estate of Sir Winston S. Churchill. © The Estate of Sir Winston S. Churchill.

YURI ANDROPOV: Courtesy of the Samantha Smith Center, Hollowell, Maine.

LOVE, DEATH & FRIENDSHIP

CICERO: *Cicero's Letters to Atticus, Vol. 4.* D. R. Shackleton-Bailey. 1966, Cambridge University Press.

ABELARD: *The Love Letters of Abelard and Heloise.* Edited by H. Morten. 1901, J. M. Dent, London.

MARY, QUEEN OF SCOTS: *Treasury of the World's Greatest Letters.* M. Lincoln Schuster. 1948, Simon and Schuster, New York.

HORATIO NELSON: *Treasury of the World's Greatest Letters.* M. Lincoln Schuster. 1948, Simon and Schuster, New York.

MARY SHELLEY: British Museum Catalogue to 1992,

Shelley Exhibition.

SIMÓN BOLÍVAR: Original Andromeda translation.

JOHN BROWN: *The Story of John Brown in his Own Words, in the Words of Those who Knew him and in the Poetry and Prose of the Literary Heritage.* Edited by Louis Ruchames. 1959, Abelard-Schuman, New York.

ABRAHAM LINCOLN: *Abraham Lincoln, Complete Works.* Edited by John G. Nicolay and John Hay. 1894, Century Co., New York.

VINCENT VAN GOGH: Original Andromeda translation.

CAPTAIN ROBERT FALCON SCOTT: *Scott's Last Expedition. The Journals.* Robert Falcon Scott. 1983, Methuen London Ltd.

CARL JUNG: *The Freud/Jung Letters.* Edited by William McGuire, translated by Ralph Mannheim and R. F. C. Hull. 1974, The Hogarth Press and Routledge and Kegan Paul.

D. H. LAWRENCE: *D. H. Lawrence's Letters of Bertrand Russell.* Edited by H. T. Moore 1948. Gotham Book Mart, New York. By kind permission of Laurence Polinger Ltd. and the Estate of Frieda Lawrence Ravagli.

FURTHER READING

800 Years of Women's Letters. Olga Kenyon and P. D. James. 1992, Alan Sutton, Stroud, U.K.
The Complete Letter-Writer in English, 1568 1800. Katherine Gee Hornbeck. 1934, Northampton, Mass.
The Faber Book of Letters: Letters written in the English language. Felix Pryor. 1988, Faber, London.
A Letter Does not Blush: a Collection of the Most Entertaining Letters in History. Nicholas Parsons. 1984.
A Letter Book: Selected with an Introduction on the History and Art of Letter-Writing. George Saintsbury. 1922, G. Bell and Sons, Ltd, London/Harcourt, Brace, New York.
Letters of the Great Artists. Richard Friedenthal. 1963,
Lost Diaries and Dead Letters. Maurice Baring. 1989, Alan Sutton, Gloucestershire, U.K.
Love Letters: an Illustrated Anthology. Antonia Fraser. 1976, 1989, Barrie and Jenkins, London.
Love Letters: an Anthology from the British Isles, 975–1944. James Turner. 1970,
Love Letters of Great Men and Women from the Eighteenth Century to the Present Day. C. H. Charles. 1924,
The Providence of Wit in the English Letter Writers. William Henry Irving. 1955, Duke University Press, N.C.
Rivals in Power: Lives and Letters of the Great Tudor Dynasties. David Starkey. 1990, Macmillan, London.
Romantic Correspondence: Women, Politics and the Fiction of Letters. Mary A. Favret. Cambridge University Press.
Second Treasury of the World's Great Letters. Wallace Brockway & Bart Keith Winer. 1950.
A Treasury of the World's Greatest Letters from Ancient Days to Our Time. M. Lincoln Schuster. 1948, Simon and Schuster, New York.
Yours Faithfully: Letters from the Famous about God, Philosophy and Religion. Jeff Thorburn. 1990, Pan.

CREDITS (ILLUSTRATIONS)

Andromeda Oxford Ltd would like to thank Richard Thomas for the germ of the idea; James Wagenvoord, Michele Perla and Deborah DeFord for their assistance, efficiency and encouragement; and Niki Moores and Claire Turner for their administrative support. Color origination by Eray Scan pte Ltd., Singapore.

159